ADDICTION AND RESPONSIBILITY

FRANCIS F. SEEBURGER

ADDICTION AND RESPONSIBILITY

AN INQUIRY INTO
THE ADDICTIVE MIND

CROSSROAD ▪ NEW YORK

Author's Acknowledgments

Portions of this book were written during leaves
granted the author by the University of Denver for the
fall quarter of 1991 and the fall quarter of 1992.
Alcoholics Anonymous World Services, Inc., is gratefully
acknowledged for permission to use material from *Alcoholics
Anonymous.*

1996
The Crossroad Publishing Company
370 Lexington Avenue, New York, NY 10017
Copyright © 1993 by Francis F. Seeburger

Library of Congress Cataloging-in-Publication Data

Seeburger, Francis F.
    Addiction and responsibility : an inquiry into the addictive mind
/ Francis F. Seeburger.
        p.   cm.
    Includes bibliographical references and index.
    ISBN 0-8245-1365-7; 0-8245-1501-3 (pbk.)
    1. Compulsive behavior.   I. Title.
RC533.S44   1993
616.86—dc20
                                          93-25168
                                          CIP

To Gayle

Contents

PART IV: Responding to Addiction

INTRODUCTION

The Philosophy of Addiction

Interest in the subject of addiction has grown remarkably in the last few decades. Popular literature on addiction has multiplied phenomenally. Bookstores across the nation now have entire sections devoted to "addiction and recovery." Television specials and segments of nightly news programs regularly address the topic. Numerous movies have been devoted either entirely or partially to it, and on any given weekend in most urban areas one can usually find some workshop on addiction or addiction-related issues to attend.

Recovery programs and treatment centers proliferate. Lecturers such as John Bradshaw and Earnie Larsen have devoted followers who flock to their lectures by the thousands, and their books spend weeks, months, or even years atop the best-seller lists. New terms such as *codependency* and *enabling* have found their way into our everyday speech.

The list of possible addictions itself seems to grow longer each day, as new addictions are continually identified (or as the behavior at issue is so labeled, at any rate). To some, America today even gives the appearance of being addicted to the idea of addiction. Accordingly, books addressing *that* addiction, under the guise of attacking the supposedly uncritical proliferation of "the addiction industry" or "addiction-treatment industry," have begun to appear in the last few years.[1]

In numerous disciplines new areas of specialization pertaining to addiction have also sprung up. Entirely new multidisciplinary fields such as alcohology have been created.

However, there is at least one field in which interest in addiction really has yet to develop—the field of philosophy. To date, professional philosophers have paid little or no serious attention to the phenomenon of addiction.[2] That is surprising, since it is difficult to imagine a realm more inviting of careful philosophical analysis.

For one thing, there is a great deal of conceptual confusion in the contemporary discussions of addiction. Above all, there is confusion concerning the very concept of addiction itself and how addiction is to be classified: as a disease, a behavior disorder, a moral failing, or what. Philosophical reflection is indispensable to dispel such confusions.

Furthermore, even though contemporary philosophers have been relatively silent about addiction, the history of philosophy itself contains many insights and suggestions that are pertinent to that topic. Since the beginning of the Western philosophical tradition among the ancient Greeks more than 2,500 years ago, philosophers have sprinkled their works with remarks relating to various aspects of addiction, though often without even using that term. A study of those as yet untapped resources can yield a wealth of material that is still valuable for us today. Paradoxically, new and fresh perspectives upon the origin, meaning, and overcoming of addiction can be laid open by the reclamation of these old riches of our own tradition.

Nor need we stop there. Beyond our own Western philosophical tradition lie other, equally great traditions. Hinduism, Islam, Confucianism, Taoism, and above all Buddhism (to mention the main examples) also have much of value to tell us concerning addiction.

By utilizing such resources, philosophical reflection upon addiction can do something even more interesting and important than helping to clarify our thinking about addiction. It can lead us to important truths about ourselves. The contemporary flowering of interest in addiction bears witness to the power of the idea of addiction to illuminate modern human life and experience. It attests that we need to integrate the phenomenon of addiction, in all its breadth and depth, into our philosophical picture of what it means to be a human being. That is necessary if we are to arrive at a comprehensive and fundamental vision of the sense of our own contemporary existence. Conversely, if we are truly to understand addiction itself, we must ultimately think of it in terms of human nature and history as a whole, and of the place of humanity within even larger wholes.

Because it addresses addiction from such a broad perspective, as well as because it is indispensable for purposes of values clarification, the philosophy of addiction is also indispensable when it comes, finally, to formulating and attempting to resolve the crucial *ethical* issues involved in addiction. There are a number of such issues. Some pertain to how the scientific study of addiction should be conducted. Others concern how addiction should be treated and prevented. Underlying both of these sets of issues is yet a third one, which includes questions of how individuals and societies should apportion responsibility for addiction and the recovery from it. We do not arrive at the real point of the philosophy of addiction (or of any other reflection on addiction, for that matter) until we finally get around to asking the fundamental ethical question of what we should *do* about addiction.

In this book, we attempt to sketch out a philosophy of addiction. We begin by asking what it is like to be addicted (Part I). We look at how addiction is experienced, both by addicts and by nonaddicts, and we examine some of the characteristic thought patterns that accompany addiction.

Next, we try to clear away some major confusions that threaten to beset our thinking about addiction, confusions pertaining to how we should define addiction, how we should categorize it, and how we should set limits to the application of the notion of addiction (Part II). We see that addiction is more than any merely physical state or group of behaviors. It is a condition that must be defined existentially—as a fundamental way in which we can *be*. That way of defining addiction allows us to justify extending the notion to cover addiction to "processes" as well as to "substances" (such as drugs or alcohol). It also shows us that we do not need to choose between viewing addiction as a disease, a behavior disorder, or even a moral failing, but that all three ways can be used to complement one another.

After that, we attempt to reach a philosophical understanding of addiction by probing its ultimate meaning and significance (Part III). We see that addiction in all its forms is a complex process of

PART I

BEING ADDICTED

·1·

The Experience of Addiction

"The question is frequently asked: Why does a man become a drug addict?" The speaker is William S. Burroughs. A highly intelligent, highly educated man, Burroughs, along with such of his friends as Jack Kerouac and Allen Ginsberg, was a founding father of the "Beat Generation." Burroughs' biography, however, is also that of a junky, an alcoholic, a nicotine addict (as, of course, are hundreds of millions of others the world over), and a habitual user of sundry other legal and illegal drugs. For years, he lived the life of active addiction, until he finally went "clean and sober" (to use a current expression).

Why *does* a man—or woman—become a drug addict?

"The answer," Burroughs continues, in sarcastic understatement, "is that he usually does not intend to become an addict. You don't wake up one morning and decide to be a drug addict."[1]

Nor does one simply wake up one morning and realize that one *is* an addict. Even after many years of heavy drug usage, addicts may insistently deny that they are addicts. They may go on denying it, even when everyone else has written them off as hopeless cases.

But what is it like to be an addict? What is it like, for example, to see one's own life "measured out in eyedroppersful of morphine solution," as Burroughs puts it for the junky?

No sooner does the thought of such a way of life (or way of death in life, as it may strike us) begin to form in our minds than most of us involuntarily recoil in horror or disgust. We regard such a life as unimaginable for people such as ourselves. We literally have trouble even imagining what it would be like, just as we who have never been through such an ordeal have trouble even imagining what it must have been like to be in Auschwitz. And we feel an aversion towards the thought of addiction, just as we do towards the thought of such horrors as the Nazi extermination camps.

Many of us have an especially strong aversive reaction of this sort when we think of addictions involving needles, syringes, and intravenous injections. We wonder "how anyone could be that way." We are aghast at the idea that anyone could sink so far below what we want to regard as the minimal level for behavior to remain comprehensibly human.

In that context, the comparison to Auschwitz again comes to mind: To those of us affected with a strong aversion to the very thought of the addict's behavior, that behavior strikes us as no more comprehensible than that of the Nazi SS gassing millions of innocent men, women, and children, while still thinking of themselves as "humane" and even "heroic."

Yet the behavior of the addict (like that of the SS, unfortunately) may not really be all that foreign to us after all. The strength of our abhorrence may testify less to how different we are from "those kinds of people" than to how uncomfortably like them we are.

At an AA meeting, an alcoholic may speak quietly of how he used to look down on the street junky, wondering how anyone could ever sink so low, to where his or her whole life narrowed down to the end of a needle. Then, he goes on, one day he finally "hit bottom" himself. That is, he was shocked into recognizing his own addiction to alcohol, and how the whole of his own life had come down to no more than the next drink. Since then, the alcoholic says in closing, he knows that he was never any better than the junky he used to look down on.

For the housewife hooked on Valium, the whole world shrinks down to the size of a little, white pill. Or think of the smoker who boasts of quitting, but who hides a pack of cigarettes somewhere around the house or in the back yard, and then devotes all of his energy to finding excuses to sneak off to have "just one more."

In the final analysis, are the lives of such persons really any less confined and confining, debased and debasing, than that of a junky in an alley opening a vein with a safety pin and squirting heroin into the hole with an eyedropper? If there is a difference worth marking, it would seem to be at most a matter of degree rather than a difference of kind. At the level of how each experiences himself or herself and the meaning of his or her life, there is little to choose between them.

Alcoholics are "restless, irritable, and discontented, unless they can experience the sense of ease and comfort which comes at once by taking a few drinks."[2] Who, if one is completely honest about it, can deny that there is something in one's own life—if not alcohol or heroin or cocaine or some prescription drug, then cigarettes or coffee or chocolate or soda, or masturbation, or even watching television or talking on the telephone—to fit that very description? For most if not all of us, there is something to which we relate as though we cannot do without it. There is something such that, if we are deprived of it, we become more and more "restless, irritable, and discontented," until and unless we can once again have whatever it is we so desperately crave. Then, once we are allowed it (or allow it to ourselves) again, we are immediately calmed and become quiet, placid, and contented.

"Fix me. Make it stop. Fix me," pleads Frankie Machine to his dealer in Nelson Algren's novel *The Man with the Golden Arm*, one of the earliest fictional depictions of narcotics addiction.[3] Who cannot identify with Frankie, at least once one gets beyond the initial, denying response of disgust and abhorrence and honestly reflects on one's own private "vices"?

"Identify, don't compare," newcomers are advised in some meetings of Alcoholics Anonymous, Narcotics Anonymous, or the like. That is also good advice to follow if we are trying to understand what it is like to be addicted. Instead of comparing our own lives negatively with those of William Burroughs or such fictional characters as Frankie Machine, attentive to all the ways in which we are not like them (a ploy at which addicts themselves, as we later consider more fully, are masters), we need to develop an eye for the ways in which we are all too like them. We need to let the light of the depiction of their experiences illuminate our own lives, permitting us to see the addictions and addictiveness present, to one degree or another, in ourselves.

Indeed, even the strength with which we reject such identification, clinging instead to our comfortably negative comparisons, reveals something of that very presence of addictiveness in our own lives. At least part of what makes us react with such abhorrence to images of the depths of addiction, refusing to admit any community with addicts who have plumbed those depths, is our hidden fear that we *are* like them, or might become so, if we relax our vigilance. Perhaps we can, in fact, all too easily imagine ourselves in their places. Perhaps that is really what frightens us so. Perhaps what most alarms us about addiction, when we respond with such aversion, is how tempted we ourselves are by it. Maybe we are so tempted—and so frightened by the fact that we are tempted—that we would even prefer actually to yield to the temptation rather than have to admit feeling it.

And that is just where our description of the experience of addiction can begin—with how *tempting* addiction is.

Addiction as Tempting

I have a friend who once tried smoking a small amount of heroin. It frightened him so much that he never tried it again. What frightened him, however, was nothing horrible about the experience. What frightened him rather, as he puts it, was that he responded so positively to the drug. He experienced the drug as telling him quite bluntly, "Get addicted to me." Seeing how easily he might do just that is what made him swear off heroin forever. (My friend's story provides a nice, inverse confirmation of Burroughs' point that addicts do not intend to become addicts.)

To be sure, not everyone who has ever taken heroin has had such an initially positive experience with it. In fact, as we discuss in more detail later, many addicts have to *learn* to enjoy taking or doing that to which they eventually become addicted. However, there is certainly a significant minority of those who become addicted to one substance or another who can attest to having responded to their first encounter with that substance much as my friend responded to his first (and only) encounter with heroin. At any rate, what is most important for our present purposes is not how one first finds one's way onto the road that ends in addiction. What matters here is only that, once on that road, if one keeps on it long enough so that one actually becomes addicted, one sooner or later comes to have experiences like my friend's. That is, one sooner or later comes to a point of being *tempted* to become addicted to the substance, process, or whatever. One experiences a temptation to *repeat* the drug taking or other behavior in a compulsive way. To yield to that temptation is, in fact, what finally leads one into addiction.

It is not just that it is tempting to use the drug or engage in the behavior to which one becomes addicted, but even more that it is tempting to use that drug or engage in that behavior *addictively*: Addiction *itself* is *tempting*.

Temptation plays a double role in addiction. In the first place, it functions in the formation of addiction. Only if there comes a point when that to which someone eventually becomes addicted (heroin, alcohol, and the like) begins to appear desirable to the addict-to-be, tempting to him or her, can addiction occur. One does not become addicted to things one is never tempted to use.

But there is also a second role for temptation to play in the experience of addiction. That is to keep the addict always coming back for more, once the addiction itself is formed.

What distinguishes the addict from the nonaddict is not a lack of will power on the part of the addict. It is not a matter of addicts being unable to withstand straightforward temptations to use a drug or engage in a practice to which nonaddicts are also drawn, but against which they exercise self-restraint. Addiction is not mere overindulgence, no matter how excessive. Such ideas fail to address the fundamental way in which addiction itself is tempting.

The proper place of addiction as such lies in the area in which the temptation is no longer merely to use some substance (or engage in some activity, if the possibility of process addiction, which we investigate later, is granted). Instead, in fully formed addiction, the temptation is to *keep on* using. It is no longer a temptation merely to use, but one to use *again and again*. The temptation is never to *stop* using.

When my friend had the feeling that the heroin he smoked was telling him, "Get addicted to me," that is just the temptation toward which he felt himself drawn: the temptation to give his whole life over to the drug. The temptation was not merely to use it, but to use it on a continuing basis, and to invest the continued usage of it with central significance in and for his life, so that nothing would take priority over using it again and again, forever.

Thus, to say that addiction is tempting does not mean merely that addiction involves being tempted to use something (some drug, for example) or to do something (act out a sexual fantasy, for example). That, of course, is true, but it is not the most important truth at issue, which is that addiction *itself* is tempting. To say that addiction is tempting means, above all, that it is tempting to *become addicted*.

In that sense, recognition of the tempting quality of addiction immediately engenders a paradox. On the one hand, as Burroughs points out, no one intends to become an addict. On the other hand, insofar as addiction itself is tempting, becoming addicted is precisely what one is tempted to do. Thus, addiction as it manifests itself in the addict's own experience is at one and the same time both unintentional and tempting.

This paradox is not unique to addiction, however. It belongs to the very nature of temptation as such. If something is such that one might choose it in full, self-reflective deliberation, then we would not speak of being "tempted" by that thing, at least in the original, strong sense of temptation. So, for example, it is only in a derivative, attenuated sense that we might speak of being tempted to love one's neighbors, or to do good to those in need.

The idea of temptation in the strong, original sense, however, involves a negative component, insofar as what tempts us must be something we experience as ultimately *un*desirable. What tempts us is that which we would *not* choose in full, self-reflective deliberation. It is that which we encounter as ultimately *not* in our own or others' best interests, something ultimately to be *avoided*.

However, what is tempting is that which, despite or even by virtue of its undesirability from the perspective of rational deliberation, nevertheless presents itself as all too desirable. The tempting is the undesirable-desired, what is desired in its very undesirability.

The addict never intends to become an addict. That is true enough (at least for the vast majority of addicts). Nor does the addict believe that the state of *addiction as such* is a good or pleasurable state, something desirable for its own sake. But that doesn't mean that there is no sense in which the addict can be said to *want* the addiction. Addiction is undesirable, even to addicts; but addicts want it anyway.

At least they want it so long as they remain in the state of "practicing" their addiction, rather than entering into a state of "recovery" from the addiction. Another friend of mine who for years battled unsuccessfully to stop smoking, before he finally managed to do so, likes to tell the story of how he once went to a hypnotherapist to help him stop. After a number of sessions, when my friend continued unabated smoking, he asked the therapist when the therapy was going to begin working. The therapist told him that first he had to *want* to quit before any therapy could have an effect. "If I wanted to quit," my friend replied, "I wouldn't need you."

Like St. Augustine praying to be relieved of his licentiousness, "only not yet," my friend did not yet want to quit smoking. To borrow a phrase from the book *Alcoholics Anonymous*, he was only to the point of "wanting to want to quit." As that same book puts it about alcoholics, "The sensation [induced in them by drinking alcohol] is so elusive that, while they admit it is injurious, they cannot after a time differentiate the true from the false."[4] They both do and do not want to drink, as well as to quit drinking.

Addiction is tempting. Becoming addicted, and then staying that way, is something that those who succumb to addiction both do and do not want to do, something they want to do even when they don't want to want to do it.

Addiction as Tranquilizing

What *makes* addiction so tempting? What is it about addiction, such that even though one will admit that being addicted is undesirable, one desires it anyway? Well, for one thing, addiction is tranquilizing. That is at least one major aspect of the temptation to become addicted.

Anyone who has ever become even moderately hooked on smoking, eating candy, watching television, or whatever, knows that condition already mentioned, the condition of being "restless, irritable, and discontented" unless one is again allowed access to the object of one's addiction. But then, when one is at last allowed the cigarette, piece of chocolate, or opportunity to switch on the TV set again, the relief is immediate. At least, that is how it is experienced, regardless of how it might look to an outside observer.

That relief may not last long. To reach or prolong it may require ever larger and more frequent "doses." The rebound after one's supply has been cut off may make one's restlessness, irritability, and discontent far worse than it ever was before one began dosing oneself. All that may well be so, but it still remains true that, when one once again reaches for that drink, that pill, that cigarette, that candy bar, that on/off switch, that sexual partner, pornographic magazine, evangelical tract, or whatever, one immediately experiences a rush of contentment and well-being. For that one fleeting moment, before whatever remorse and horror may be waiting just past it, everything is all right again. God's in His heaven; all's right with the world.

"Fix me. Make it stop. Fix me."

And the fixer does, for at least that one moment and whatever the price to be paid later.

The deeper one sinks into addiction, the more desperate becomes the pain and agitation and need when one is deprived of that to which one has become addicted, and the greater is the eventual sense of relief when that deprivation is lifted. Thus, as with temptation, tranquilization plays a role not only in the initial formation of addiction but also and even more emphatically in the continuance and worsening of addiction as an experienced dependency.

At the level of the addict's own experience of addiction, the relationship between tranquilization and dependency is a direct one. The greater the degree of experienced tranquilization through "practicing" the addiction, the greater is the degree of experienced dependency. At the same time, the greater the experienced dependency, the greater is the sense of tranquilization that comes from practicing the addiction.

Addiction as Disburdening

We uncovered the tranquilizing quality of addiction by deepening our questioning about its tempting quality. In the same way, by deepening our questioning about this second characteristic (tranquilization), we can uncover yet another experiential characteristic of addiction.

What makes addiction so tranquilizing is above all that it relieves us of responsibility for ourselves and our lives.

When the addict is practicing his or her addiction, then the addict's life becomes extremely simple. If that life can be measured out in eyedroppersful of heroin solution or shots of whiskey, then that life itself has become wholly clarified. All questions of meaning, goal, and direction have been answered. All matters of priorities have been settled. All tensions have been resolved.

Here is a first-person account of a compulsive stock-market gambler:

> There definitely was a high with it, a very enthusiastic feeling. But in a way it was also a distraction. It took me out of my present reality. I didn't think about any of the problems in my life while I was watching that ticker. It was a release from other things, kept my mind busy, and took it off everything else. It gave me something to focus on.[5]

What addiction distracts me from is my own life. In such distraction, it relieves me of the burden of that life, of actually having to live it out, with all the uncertainty, boredom, routine, frustration, and disappointment that so often characterize even the most fortunate life. Most especially, addiction relieves me of the need to keep on searching for meaning in my life, the need to *give* my own life meaning through commitment, dedication, and daily perseverance. Thanks to my addiction, the search is over. I no longer have to give my own life meaning. My addiction gives it meaning. My addiction *is* the meaning.

Practicing an addiction becomes an all-consuming activity. The time involved in actually taking the drug or engaging in the addictive behavior is only a small part of the total amount of time devoted to the addiction. Time spent securing the supply of the drug or the opportunity to act out some behavioral compulsion, time spent planning to use or act out, time spent anticipating the results, time spent arranging all of the trappings and rituals one has built into using the drug or performing the action—time spent on these and all the other activities that go with the addiction must also be taken into account. When they are, it is easy to see how the addict's addiction can come to fill up the entirety of the addict's life, squeezing out all else.

Indeed, this aspect of addiction can be dramatically present even when relatively little time is devoted to indulgence in the actual core addictive habit itself. So, for example, on most days a given alcoholic may confine drinking to no more than a single cocktail before dinner, with more excessive consumption consigned to occasional "binges." Nevertheless, the alcoholic's entire day can be centered around that one daily drink. It can be the goal toward which the entire day is directed, the first thing one thinks of in the morning, a promise the recollection of which gives one constant solace throughout working hours, an ever-present distraction causing one to make a series of minor mistakes throughout the day, a moment the anticipation of which is all that keeps one going. Then, once that magic moment finally arrives and passes, one can be thrown into restlessness and irritability, an impatient waiting for bedtime to arrive so one can get the night behind one and begin it all again the next morning. Day after day can go by in that same way, mounting into years. In a grim parody of the slogan "one day at a time," the addict's life goes on in that fashion long after all the life has been drained out of it.

That is a heavy price to pay. The reward for paying it, however, is that the addict no longer has to bear the burden of any other debts. By paying the price of having one's life reduced to the size of a shot glass or hypodermic needle, the addict is released from the necessity of having to live.

Life ceases to be a burden once one turns it over to one's addiction. It ceases to require decisions, since all decisions have already been made. All that's left to do is to carry out, over and over and over again, the same ritualized behaviors leading to the same ritualized results. The addiction now lives one's life for one, disburdening one of it.

A person who hears the appeal of such an offer has a vocation for addiction.

Addiction as Entangling

At least in part, what allows addiction to disburden the addict of all responsibility for life—responsibility for making decisions and paying the consequences—is yet another of its experiential characteristics, its *entangling* quality. In a variety of ways, addiction has the capacity to entangle addicts in their own addictions, to wrap them ever more tightly in its threads, until they eventually vanish within the addiction itself.

It is largely by way of such entanglement that addiction can disburden us. If addiction had no power to catch the addict up in its own convolutions, then it would not be able to interpose itself between the addict and the addict's own life. It would not be able to color every aspect of that life, becoming an all-consuming passion. It could not absorb all the addict's attention, as it must if it is to disburden the addict of the need to pay attention to anything else.

Viewed from the outside, the addict's life is entirely made up of trivia. From such a perspective, the high brought on for a moment by the use of the addictive substance or the performance of the addictive activity is all but blocked from view by the mass of routine, mechanical, ritualistic, repetitive behaviors that make up the bulk of the addict's day. All of the addict's effort and attention must first be directed toward locating the drug dealer, gullible physician, open liquor store, prostitute, or other "source" for the addictive object. Then, once the source is located, the addict must do whatever is necessary to avail himself or herself of it. Often, that takes up the lion's share of the addict's time—the stealing, begging, borrowing, pleading, conning, and conniving necessary to obtain the financial and other means to keep feeding the addiction. Only if that enterprise proves successful can contact with the source be made and a "supply" be secured. Even then it still remains necessary to find a safe way and place to "use." Assuming that all obstacles can be overcome, and the addict finally gets his or her "fix," the desired effects last only a relatively short time. Then the whole process must begin again.

It is not just the next fix that the addict is intent upon. What counts, finally, is to get that fix in such a way as not to endanger ongoing access to the supply. One fix is never enough. The goal is to ensure an unbroken continuity of fixes.

However, the more one practices the addiction, the more complex and devious become the ways one must go to ensure that one can continue to practice it. The more one secures the supply, the more new threats arise, demanding ever new responses. The more lies one tells to protect the addiction, the more lies one has to tell. There is a perpetual escalation of entanglements until, at last, the very possibility of extricating oneself vanishes altogether from view. At that point, the entanglement is so complete that the addict may even abandon all pretense. All lies and deviousness may be dropped, and one may begin practicing one's addiction in complete openness.

Of course, abandoning all pretenses also means abandoning all hope. It means turning oneself completely over to the addiction. Now, there is a total response to the addictive call: One abandons oneself utterly to it.

Addiction at every stage involves the total person, but only now does it involve the person totally.[6] That is, addiction always involves the whole of the addict's life, affecting all aspects of that life in some fashion and to some degree; but only here, in the most extreme form of addiction, does the addict totally submit to the addiction.

Addiction *involves* the addict. It does not present itself as some externally imposed condition. Instead, it comes toward the addict as the addict's very self. The addict is wholly involved in the addiction, completely wrapped up in it—enrapt by it.

Contrary to what appears to be the case from the external perspective mentioned previously, the rapture of addiction is not at all confined to those few moments when the addict is actually engaging in the addictive practice (taking the drug, performing the action). "Rapture" is literally the state of being taken and held outside of oneself, and the addict is enrapt by addiction throughout the entire process leading up to "using," then leading back to it again and again. In fact, it is the very rigidity and repetitiveness of addiction, the fact of circling back again time after time after time to the same invariant point, that makes up the rapturous nature of addiction. It is precisely this repetitive sameness of addiction that takes one so completely outside of oneself.

Addiction as Alienating

The rapture to be found in the entanglement of addiction is not an enriching rapture. The loss of self in addiction is not a paradoxical way of finding oneself, as it can be in religious rapture, for example. When one loses oneself to an addiction, one loses the very chance of finding oneself at all.

Addiction is *alienating*. That is another of its experiential characteristics.

We sometimes speak of being alienated from our families,

friends, or communities; and in some cases "alienation of affections" is still grounds for naming a third party in a divorce suit. Addiction is certainly alienating in both of those senses. It divides families, separates friends, and fragments communities. And it is difficult to imagine anything more able to alienate affections: addiction demands priority in the addict's emotional life and constantly tries to take sole possession of the addict's heart.

However, addiction is alienating in a far more fundamental way than that. The root of all alienation is alienation from oneself. To "alienate" means literally to make foreign to ... alien to.... In common English the term *alienation* means the same thing as *estrangement*. To estrange is to make strange to ... to make a stranger to....

Addiction makes strangers of wives to husbands and husbands to wives, of parents to children and children to parents, and of neighbors to neighbors. More importantly, it makes one a stranger to oneself.

Addiction robs one of oneself. It deprives one of the ownership of one's own life. That life ceases to be "one's own" and becomes nothing more than an expression of the underlying addiction. Genuine creativity is gone, and with it goes any real opportunity for self-expression. All of the addict's behavior comes to manifest the addiction, rather than any uniqueness of the addicted person or that person's rich individual inheritance.

By disburdening addicts of responsibility for living their own lives, addiction also wipes out any claims addicts themselves can make to those lives. Since their lives are claimed entirely by their addictions, addicts themselves must relinquish all claims of their own. They have no rights over their own lives any longer. Having become like unaffected parties attempting to assert themselves into a civil suit, they no longer have any "standing" to assert such rights.

All other ways in which addiction is alienating follow from this fundamental self-alienation, this fundamental estrangement from oneself. To enter into any genuine relationship with others, for example, requires first of all that one have a firm sense of self. Otherwise, there is nothing there to serve as an anchor in the relationship. When the self is no longer one's own, one cannot genuinely give of oneself to another.

Thus, as alienated from themselves addicts are also inevitably alienated from others. They cannot participate as fully functioning independent members of a family, group, or society. No longer there for themselves, they cannot be there for anyone else, either. Having lost individual independence, they have also lost the capacity for any genuine interdependence with others.

The only time the addict feels all right is when pursuing the addiction. How could it be otherwise? Since the addiction has taken over property rights to the self, that is the only time addicts experience themselves as "belonging." And they are right: dispossessed of themselves, addicts belong solely to their addictions.

Being alienated from themselves by their addictions, addicts feel that they are being themselves only when indulging those addictions. The only sense of self they have left is what they experience when engaging in their addictive practices. Similarly, the only company with whom they feel at home is the company of other addicts. That is the only fellowship left to them.

Addiction as Self-Dissembling

It is a common occurrence for those whose families are disturbed by their loved ones' drinking or drug taking to deny that they have any problem, when confronted with the family's worries about their behavior. In Alcoholics Anonymous or other self-help groups, one often hears it said that alcoholism or some other given addiction is "a disease of denial." Various members of the group may talk about how they were "in denial" throughout all the years of practicing their addictions. Or they may talk about how friends or relatives who are still practicing their own addictions are "in denial." Someone may remark that alcoholism, or addiction in general, is "the only disease that tells you you don't have it."

We consider the idea that addiction is a disease later. Here, all that we take from such remarks is the notion of "denial."

That specific term *denial* belongs within the horizon of a basically psychological perspective upon addiction. It suggests that addicts erect mental defense mechanisms to guard themselves against having to acknowledge their addictions, much as persons suffering severe traumas may erect such defenses against recollecting the traumatic episode.

In the case of a severely traumatic occurrence, the memory of the event may be too painful for the mind to accept. In the same way, according to the view implicit in the use of the term *denial*, to have to acknowledge that one is an addict may be too painful for the addict. The addict's sense of self-esteem may be too fragile to accept such a label.

Another factor that may contribute to erecting such supposed defense mechanisms is thought to be the desire to continue the addictive practice. By denying that one is an addict, the idea goes, one can protect oneself against having to stop the addictive behavior. In that way denial would be a mechanism in the service of "protecting the supply."

However it is finally to be conceptualized (whether psychologically in terms of such mechanisms of "denial," or in some other terms), the experiential characteristic of addiction at issue behind such conceptualization is important to note. It is the characteristic of being *self-dissembling*.

Addiction manifests itself in the addict's experience as something other than addiction. That is its self-dissembling character. By dissembling itself addiction conceals from the addict its own nature and, therewith, the addict's condition as addict as well.

In brief, the structure of such dissembling involves a sort of peep show in which addiction simultaneously reveals and conceals its own characteristics. Thus, as they experience their own states, addicts will simultaneously hold incompatible views of themselves. On the one hand, for example, they will acknowledge that their temptation to "pick up" and "use" is sometimes "irresistible." At the same time, however, those same addicts may bristle at the slightest suggestion that they are not "in control" of their own behavior. They will insist, against any such suggestions, that they are making deliberate decisions to use each time they do so.

Or, to give another example, addicts will acknowledge they have become so entangled in lies and pretenses in the service of their addictions that they can no longer see any way to extricate themselves, while nevertheless insisting that the practice of their addictions is an assertion of their freedom. Or they will complain of how isolated and alienated they feel, yet experience any threat to their addictions as an attack upon their inviolable personal rights.

"I'm not hooked; I can quit any time I want to," says the smoker, reaching for another cigarette when the one lighted only moments ago still sits burning in the ashtray, or even in the smoker's hand. That and similar images have long been stereotypes of popular culture. They give unmistakable testimony to the self-dissembling character of addiction.

The preceding five experiential characteristics of addiction already play into this sixth one of dissembling itself. Thus, the alienating character of addiction is masked by its tranquilizing quality, and the former disguises the latter. The entanglements that go with addiction cover up not only its other aspects but also its very entangling character itself. And temptation, by its very nature, is already self-dissembling. Each characteristic helps to hide one or all of the others, even when it doesn't hide itself.

In return, the self-dissembling characteristic of addiction heightens each of addiction's other characteristics. The more self-dissembling the addiction, the more it entangles addicts and alienates them from themselves, to a point where they can no longer find their way back to any genuine self at all. Equally, however, the more addiction dissembles itself, the more it is able to dissemble the cares and worries that beset addicts, tranquilizing and disburdening them of all their concerns.

Addiction as Self-Perpetuating

A seventh and final experiential characteristic of addiction becomes most glaringly evident in addicts' experience of addiction when they try to overcome their addictive behaviors. On such occasions, when addicts try to break free of their addictions, they experience a stubborn resistance to all their attempts to change. Especially at such times, those addictions manifest themselves as *self-perpetuating*.

Willpower's Not Enough, proclaims the title of a recent book about addiction.[7] That title itself is borrowed from the remarks to that effect made every day by countless addicts themselves in meetings of AA and other self-help groups around the country and most of the rest of the world. The same idea is driven home in passage after passage of *Alcoholics Anonymous*, the "basic text" for AA and, through it, for the whole "twelve-step" movement (the self-help movement that models itself on AA and its "Twelve Steps" for recovery from alcoholism).

Addicts everywhere know the experience. Time after time, they have resolved "never again," only to find themselves months, days, or even hours later violating those resolutions. Nor are such resolutions mere pretenses. Rather, the addicts who make them frequently do so with the greatest conviction and sense of commitment. They make their resolutions with every intention and desire to keep them. The sincerity of the addicts' resolve can be accepted as evident by their family and friends, not merely by the addicts themselves.

At least that is how it is at the time such resolutions are first made. But those resolutions soon crumble. Or, to capture addicts' self-experience more adequately, the resolutions themselves may remain as strong as ever; but they seem to be of no effect. Despite all such resolutions, often no sooner than they are made, the addict "uses" again.

On such occasions, addiction seems to take on a life of its own, independent of the desires and decisions of the addict. It is as if the addiction were an external force acting inexorably on the addict, as inexorably as an avalanche sweeps over whomever is unfortunate enough to be in its way. In such experiences, the alienation of addicts from themselves through their own addictions reaches its culmination, as does their entanglement in those addictions. Now, addiction appears to those who are addicted as a doom or a fatality from which escape no longer seems possible. Having begun by being tempted into addiction, at this point the addict himself or herself seems to vanish altogether. Only the addiction seems to remain.

·2·

The Addictive Mind

The Circularity of Addictive Thinking

One of the planets "the little prince" visits, in Antoine de Saint-Exupéry's fairy tale classic of that name, is inhabited by "a tippler." The little prince asks the tippler what he is doing. The tippler replies that he is drinking. When the little prince asks why he is drinking, the tippler says he drinks so that he may forget. "Forget what?" asks the little prince. "Forget that I am ashamed," replies the tippler. Feeling sorry for the tippler and wanting to help, the little prince then asks the tippler what he is ashamed of. "Ashamed of drinking," the tippler responds.[1]

In less than a page Saint-Exupéry thus captures something of the essence of the alcoholic mind. Indeed, he thereby manages to capture something of the essence of addictive thinking in general. Such thinking turns in upon itself in just such absurd ways as the tippler's—ways that, perhaps precisely because of their complete absurdity, allow the addict no possibility of escape from his or her addiction.

The more alcoholics drink, the more shame they feel; the more shame they feel, the more they drink to forget that shame, or at least to make it bearable. The more compulsive overeaters eat, the fatter they grow; the fatter they grow, the more disgusting they find themselves to be, and the more they turn to food in search of comfort in the face of that self-disgust. The more compulsive gamblers gamble, the deeper into debt they go, and the more they **gam-**

ble to pay off those debts. The examples can be multiplied throughout the entire range of addictive behaviors.

Addicts find themselves caught in the circle of their own thoughts. Their addictions justify themselves by appeal to the very conditions those addictions have engendered. Then those same conditions are worsened by the continued pursuit of the addiction, which in turn justifies even further intensification of the addictive behavior.

Why addicts allow themselves to become trapped in such circularities of thought will remain open here. Various accounts have been proposed to answer that question. Whatever theoretical explanation might eventually vanquish the others (if any one of them ever does), however, the phenomenon itself is undeniable.

There is also something immediately understandable about it. Indeed, it may be that at least this aspect of addictive thinking is so inherently intelligible that the very endeavor to "explain" it through elaborate theories should itself be regarded as just one more instance of stubbornly circular addictive thinking. Aristotle's ancient observation that a mark of education is knowing when to stop asking for explanations may well apply here.

Thought can feed upon itself. We all know that from our own experience. Addicts or not, we have all been caught in circularities of reasoning no less glaring than the one that catches up Saint-Exupéry's tippler. And we all know what it is like, once caught in such a circle, to be unable to escape no matter how hard we struggle.

We also all know how absurd our entrapment seems to us, once something has sprung the circle open and set us free. Then, when we look back, it is "beyond us" how we could have let ourselves fall prey to such a "silly mistake." We laugh at ourselves and shake our heads. It is like an inverse of those drawings for children in which one at first cannot pick out the figure of some animal cleverly concealed amidst the foliage, then the figure suddenly forms before the eyes, and one can no longer *not* see it there. What had so recently (when we were still caught, spinning endlessly around in our circling thoughts) been crystal clear to us, but apparently incomprehensible to others, now suddenly becomes incomprehensible to us as well.

Until, that is, we again get caught up in the whirl of the same "mistake" or of some other one just as absurd. Then the whole pattern repeats itself. Again we can imagine no other way to think than within the confines of the circle, until we are once again freed from it, and it becomes incomprehensible once more. Like the reversing polarities of alternating electrical current, the comprehensible and the incomprehensible switch positions back and forth.

Thus, when they are thinking addictively, addicts cannot understand any other way of thinking. Their addictive thoughts are obvious to them, and among themselves they ridicule outsiders who do not understand. That anyone might think differently than addicts themselves do, strikes them not merely as strange, but even as outlandishly so—an impossible possibility, so far as they can relate to it at all.

Once they have overcome their addictions, however, those same addicts find their own earlier way of thinking no less outlandish than they used to find "straight" patterns of thought. At least that is how it often appears to addicts on the surface. However, addicts' own subsequent experiences of the recurrence of addictive thought patterns, even after long periods of abstinence, suggest that the old habits of thinking continue to lie just below the surface, waiting to be reactivated.

Seemingly without any awareness it is happening, addicts slip back into their addictions. They do not realize anything is wrong until it is too late. Later, when they break out of the circle once again and look back over their own experience, they repeatedly see that, before the explicitly addictive behavior even began to resurface, the old patterns of thought had prepared the way.

But how can one control one's own thoughts? The harder the addict tries to do so, the more subtly do the apparently vanquished addictive thoughts insinuate themselves into the addict's mind, until they once again become dominant. There seems to be no way out. The circle keeps closing.

"Without Defense Against the First Drink"

If one never takes a drink, one won't ever get drunk. What could be simpler? By such logic, all alcoholics need to do to overcome their drinking problem is to practice careful abstinence from all alcohol. All they need to do is avoid ever taking that "first drink."

Of course, the alcoholic must become sufficiently motivated to take such a step; but once the motivation is there, it is just a matter of carrying out the intention. As at least one newspaper editorial put it only a few years ago, what alcoholics need to quit drinking is just "compassion and motivation."[2] If alcoholics really can be motivated to quit—if they really can be brought to the point of genuinely *wanting* to quit—then surely they *can* do so. After all, as many members of Alcoholics Anonymous themselves say, no one ever held them down and forced alcohol down their throats. Every drink they ever drank they reached for with their own hands.

Furthermore, if such reasoning works for the alcoholic, then it should also work for other addictions. Surely the key is motivation. Only if there is something about addiction that renders the addict defenseless against the addiction itself would such reasoning be discredited.

That, however, is precisely how it seems to addicts in their own experience of their addictions: that they are rendered defenseless in just such a way. Alcoholics, for example, often report experiencing their alcoholism that way. To use the language of the book *Alcoholics Anonymous*, they experience themselves as "without defense against the first drink."[3]

Some of the examples from *Alcoholics Anonymous* have become classics. One concerns a man identified simply as "Jim." After years of battling the bottle, including trips to the sanatorium, business difficulties, and domestic upset, Jim thought that he had at last won the war. Thanks to contact with members of the newly emerging fellowship that was soon to become known as AA, he had accepted that he was not supposed to drink at all, and had managed to put together a number of weeks of abstinence. His business as a car salesman was again starting to go well, and he had regained his self-respect. Jim seemed at last to have found his path. Then, however, as told in the book,

> . . . he got drunk again. We asked him to tell us exactly how it happened. This is his story: "I came to work on Tuesday morning. I remember I felt irritated that I had to be a salesman for a concern I once owned. I had a few words with the boss, but nothing serious. Then I decided to drive into the country and see one of my prospects for a car. On the way I felt hungry so

I stopped at a roadside place where they have a bar. I had no intention of drinking. I just thought I would get a sandwich. I also had the notion that I might find a customer for a car at this place, which was familiar for I had been going to it for years. I had eaten there many times during the months I was sober. I sat down at a table and ordered a sandwich and a glass of milk. Still no thought of drinking. I ordered another sandwich and decided to have another glass of milk.

"*Suddenly the thought crossed my mind that if I were to put an ounce of whiskey in my milk it couldn't hurt me on a full stomach. I ordered a whiskey and poured it into the milk. I vaguely sensed that I was not being any too smart, but felt reassured as I was taking the whiskey on a full stomach.* The experiment went so well that I ordered another whiskey and poured it into more milk. That didn't seem to bother me so I tried another."

Thus started one more journey to the asylum for Jim.[4]

Nor is it only alcoholics who tell such stories. Here is another, this time from a cigarette smoker. G. Alan Marlatt, an expert in the treatment of addiction and compulsive behaviors who specializes in "relapse prevention," could not prevent his own relapse into smoking as he describes it in the following incident. All of his knowledge of the field did him no good when it came to his own case and his nicotine addiction. Having been off cigarettes for "several months," Marlatt arrived at the airport for a business trip and went to the counter for his seat reservation. Here is how Marlatt describes what followed (which occurred when smoking in designated sections of the airplane was still permitted after takeoff):

> "Smoker or nonsmoker?" asked the clerk. Although I had not consciously thought about smoking in several weeks, I replied: "It really doesn't matter so long as I get a window seat on the right side of the plane." The clerk checked the computer and said, "I have only one window seat left on that side—but it's in the smoking section." "That'll be fine," I said.
> ... while the "you are now free to smoke" announcement was being made [once the plane was airborne] (presumably endorsed by an authority no less than the Captain himself, since it was he who turned off the no smoking sign) the man sitting next to me immediately pulled out a pack of Camels. Along

with almost everyone else in the smoking section, he lit a cigarette and took a deep, satisfying drag. All around me, folks were flicking their Bics and I was soon surrounded by the familiar pale blue cloud. Since I was still vulnerable to the old familiar aromas of tobacco smoke, the cloud filled my head with positive outcome expectancies. My neighbor, observing that I was the only person in rows 21–35 [the designated smoking section] who was *not* smoking, turned to me and said, "Would you care for one?" He offered his pack, a cigarette jutting out enticingly waiting to be plucked. A quick rationalization passed through my mind: "Why not? Just one won't hurt. Besides, I deserve it—I have been working hard for days reviewing grant applications and this is my first chance to relax." "Well, thanks, I don't mind if I do," I said to my friendly companion. As with many smokers in these days of considerable antismoking sentiment, he seemed pleased with my response, as if I had communicated a sense of common brotherhood in our mutual addiction, and offered me a light. While smoking the cigarette, my mind came up with additional rationalizations in an attempt to cope with the guilt . . . I experienced: "Well, it's okay to do this under these special circumstances. Let's make a specific exception to the no smoking rule—while it is still not permitted to smoke while I'm on the ground, it's okay to have a cigarette now and then while I'm flying; as soon as touchdown occurs, that's it, no more." Later that day, I found myself making the following pitch: "Actually, I think it is permissible to smoke for a day or two during this trip, but only while I'm out of state. Washington, D.C. is okay since no one here really knows me, but smoking in Washington State is definitely out." And so on, until I had made enough "special exceptions" that almost any event, place, or time was covered. In all, it was several weeks before I was again off the weed.[5]

To paraphrase a line from *Alcoholics Anonymous*, nonsmokers may find Marlatt's behavior incomprehensible, but unhappy smokers will understand. In my own case, I had once been off cigarettes for an entire year. I only rarely had so much as the thought of a cigarette cross my mind. Then one day I was making preparations for a family trip. (Does getting ready for a trip perhaps have some mysterious connection with such relapses?) We were leaving from Colorado to drive to New Jersey the next day, to visit my wife's parents. I was alone at home, trying to get the house clean before we left, when I came across a small bit of a leftover plug of chewing tobacco.

Like many smokers with a long history of efforts to control their nicotine addiction, I had often experimented with other ways of using tobacco besides smoking cigarettes. I had tried cigars, a pipe, snuff, and chewing tobacco, sometimes sequentially and sometimes simultaneously, in various failed endeavors to wean myself from cigarettes. I thoroughly enjoyed them all, and invariably ended up using them right along with my daily minimum of three packs of cigarettes (until my finances could no longer stand the added strain, and I would cut back to just the cigarettes).

I found the chewing tobacco inside my otherwise empty pipe-tobacco humidor. I no longer remember what reason I gave myself for nosing around in the humidor in the first place. I probably told myself that I wanted to be thorough in my cleaning. Anyway, the bit of chewing tobacco was so small that a less meticulous cleaner would have overlooked it. It was hard as a rock.

I sniffed it. I wondered what it would taste like. Surely such a small amount wouldn't matter. After all, chewing tobacco had not even been my preferred way of taking the drug. And I had been off cigarettes for a whole year. What could it hurt? Just to be on the safe side, I wouldn't even take it all, even small as it was. I managed to chisel off the merest dot with a knife and stuck it in my mouth between my teeth and my gums.

I made it to the middle of Kansas the next day before I had to pull off the Interstate and buy chewing tobacco. The convenience store didn't have plug, so I settled for leaf.

It took me a few months before I was back up to three packs of cigarettes a day. That, however, was not for lack of wanting. Then it took me six more years of smoking before I was finally able to kick the habit again.

Jim's, Marlatt's, and my episodes have a number of common features. In all of them, the addict had been able successfully to abstain for a considerable period of time prior to the relapse. In all, the relapse was prepared for and initiated by peculiar patterns of thinking, patterns in which distortions of thought allow for the minimization of situational risks and the dangers of a return to usage. In each of the cases there is also a significant element of what we might call "magic" thinking: the idea that one can, in effect, immunize oneself against the effects of a drug by introducing irrelevant, quasi-ritualistic factors into one's usage. Thus, Jim thinks to himself that whiskey can't possibly affect him if he just mixes it with milk and drinks on a full stomach; Marlatt rationalizes that it is all right to smoke again so long as he confines it to occasions when he is flying, or out of town, or in some other "special" situation; I assure myself that dried-out chewing tobacco is all right because it was cigarettes that were always my downfall (conveniently forgetting that my own past history put the lie to any such idea).

It is as if addicts have lost the capacity to generalize across situations, when it comes to their addictions. The ability to learn from our own past experience requires that we discern similarities between earlier situations and new ones as they arise. It demands that we recognize analogies and functional equivalencies between situations that may differ markedly in their details. Otherwise, given any two situations that are not identical in all regards (which means given any two situations at all), we will not see any possibility of applying what we learned in the first situation to the second. We would have to relearn how to tie our shoelaces each time we bought a new pair or shoes, or even a new pair of laces—if we didn't have to relearn it each time we put on our old shoes with their old laces, because the scuffs they had picked up since we tied them the last time made them appear to us as totally unfamiliar objects. (Indeed, we would daily have to relearn what shoes were, so far as that goes.)

When it is a matter of their addictions, however, that is just the predicament in which addicts often seem to find themselves. So, for example, despite the fact that his past experiences with drinking had demonstrated with blunt brutality that he should stay away from alcohol altogether, Jim innocently assumed that *this* time was different, because he is mixing it with milk and consuming it on a full stomach. Or Marlatt assured himself that being in an airplane soaring through the air meant that what has always applied to cigarettes for him before did not apply on *this* occasion.

Commenting upon some of the more outlandish things philosophers have all too often asserted with vehement insistence, the twentieth-century philosopher Ludwig Wittgenstein once expressed wonder at what he took to be philosophy's peculiar power to blind us to the obvious. Perhaps the solution to Wittgenstein's puzzlement lies not in the nature of philosophy as such, but in some as yet undiagnosed form of thought addiction to which philosophers (if not all academics) are especially prone. At any rate, such examples as those of Jim and Marlatt show that the risk of being blinded to the obvious is not unique to philosophers.

"I Can Handle It"

Nor is it only when they relapse that addicts appear to suffer from such blindness. Blindness to the obvious also often manifests itself in the experience of addicts before they ever get to a point of having the privilege of relapsing—before, that is, they ever "swear off" or abstain in the first place. Indeed, many addicts never attempt to kick their habits at all, but continue to practice their addictions throughout their lives. They never even formulate an intention to quit, let alone actually try to do so, only to find themselves relapsing into their addictions.

Practicing their addictions may result in disasters for addicts personally, financially, and professionally. They may lose their families, possessions, and jobs to their addictions. They may lose friends, acquaintances, and the respect of their neighbors. They may lose their driver's licenses and their freedom. They may lose their health, both mental and physical. Yet they may still go on practicing their addictions, wondering why their luck is so bad and scheming how they can regain all they have lost, without it ever occurring to them to put the blame where it really belongs or to try quitting their drinking or drugging or other addictive behavior. Finally, they may even lose their very lives to their addictions, still refusing to entertain the notion that the fault might be in themselves rather than in their stars.

The image of the alcoholic dying on the hospital bed, insisting to the end that he can "handle it" (the "it" being his drinking) has become a cliché. Nevertheless, numerous alcoholics have gone to just such extremes. And many more can easily imagine themselves having done so, "but for the grace of God" or whatever other "higher power" they credit for bringing about the "personality change" referred to in *Alcoholics Anonymous*—the change "suffi-cient to bring about recovery from alcoholism."[6]

Of course, alcoholism is not the only addiction which can lead to death. So can addiction to heroin, morphine, other narcotics, and such nonnarcotic drugs as cocaine. Nicotine addiction is the worst offender, for that matter. Cigarette smoking brings about far more deaths annually than even alcohol does, even if one counts fatalities from alcohol-related accidents and the like. The image of the man or woman still struggling to force the smoke into his or her devastated lungs as he or she lies dying, sometimes even coughing up parts of those lungs between puffs, is an even more gruesome variant of the same theme as the dying alcoholic who can still handle it.

Nor can the death toll be confined to addictions involving drugs or alcohol. Well-publicized cases such as that of Karen Carpenter have made the potentially fatal results of such eating disorders as anorexia nervosa, which is often treated as belonging to the cate-gory of addictive behaviors and which at least one expert classifies as an "aversive addiction,"[7] common knowledge. "Love addic-tions" and "relationship addictions" can also lead to death, as when an abused woman stays in an abusive relationship through beating after beating, until the last one finally kills her.

In the case of all these addictions or addiction-like behaviors, addicts will often literally die first, before admitting their addictions to themselves and seeking out whatever help they need to overcome them. Like rabbits struck motionless by the headlights of the auto-mobile that is about to run them over, such addicts seem to be held in thrall by the very addictions that are killing them.

That all too common phenomenon has come to be known by the popular term *denial*. As remarked in the preceding chapter, although that term as it has come to be used in the literature about addiction conceals an at least implicit *theory* of addiction, it still marks something the occurrence of which is undeniable.

Both this "I can handle it" feature and the preceding feature of addictive thinking exemplified by the alcoholics' seemingly being "without defense against the first drink" involve what might best be described as selective perception. In cases of addicts "using" again despite their efforts to maintain abstinence, addicts allow themselves to become charmed, as it were, by the trivial differences between past and present situations, enabling them to overlook obvious similarities that would warn them away from the impending "abstinence violation," as Marlatt labels it. Such a fascination with situational differences conveniently (conveniently, that is, for the continuance of their addictive behaviors) provides addicts with ready rationalizations for doing again whatever it is they have supposedly sworn off ever doing again (drinking, smoking, and the like). It allows them to fall prey once more to the illusion that "this time" will be different.

In the same way, addicts who insist even to the grave that they have the ability to "handle it" also display a fascination with differences. Here, however, it is not so much differences between past and present situations that bewitch addicts. Rather, it is the differences between various individuals who find themselves *in* those situations. Thus, for example, those who cannot keep a job because of their drinking and who have a history of alcohol-related traffic offenses will resist any suggestion that they have an alcohol problem by pointing out all the ways in which they are "different."

In AA parlance, such individuals are often said to be suffering from the condition of "terminal uniqueness." They are acutely aware of all the ways in which they are, or at least take themselves to be, unlike other individuals, those very ones who need to quit drinking or whatever and seek help. "I can't be an alcoholic because I never drink in the morning"—or "at work," "before an important engagement," "to get rid of a hangover," or the like. "I can't be an addict because I've never been fired from a job"—or "lost my family," "wrecked my car," or any of the other possible variants. The list is endless. There is always some difference to be found between oneself and those "others"—those alcoholics, junkies, or other addicts.

At the same time, there is a second selectivity of perception at work in the "I can handle it" phenomenon. It is closely related to the one just considered, which selects out the differences between individuals in preference to the similarities between them. This second selectivity involves a preference for what we might call psychological self-assessment over behavioral self-assessment.

By assessing oneself psychologically we mean judging oneself in terms of such things as one's conscious motives or intentions in performing given actions. In contrast, to assess oneself behaviorally would be to do so in terms of those actions themselves. For example, if I were to think of myself as a good teacher because I felt a strong commitment to teaching, deep concern about my students, and enduring motivation to help them learn, then I would be using a psychological self-assessment. On the other hand, if I were to support my claim to be a good teacher by pointing, say, to the time I spent in preparation, grading, individual tutoring, and actual classroom teaching, I would be relying on a behavioral self-assessment.

In any genuinely critical self-assessment, of course, attention would need to be paid to both factors. Most of the time most of us prefer one over the other, however. All too often, what determines our preference is simply which of the two will make us come out looking the best. Thus, most of us are versed in switching back and forth between psychological and behavioral bases of self-assessment, as circumstances dictate. For instance, when I inadvertently offend someone, what "really" counts are my intentions; but intentions suddenly sink in my esteem when I am the one who takes offense.

At least in that regard, addicts as a class are probably no different from the rest of us: when faced with a choice between self-assessments that will make them feel good about themselves and those that will make them feel not so good, they have a tendency to choose the former. If the addicted among us differ from the nonaddicted, it is surely not insofar as addicts have such a tendency.

The tendency at issue most often manifests itself in the form of a preference for psychological over behavioral self-assessment. That is especially easy to understand in the case of the addict, since it is precisely the addictive behavior that has to become problematic, if the question of a negative self-assessment as an "addict" is ever to arise. The addict's drinking or drugging or the equivalent must bring about results that are somehow damaging to the addict, even if only to the addict's reputation.

A recent antidrug television commercial shows a father discovering his young son's "stash." Confronting the son, the father asks him where he ever learned about doing such things. "I learned it from you," the son replies.

"Do what I say, not what I do—and judge me on that basis, too!" That might well be used as the addict's motto, if it did not, unfortunately, fit a far broader class. Here again, the addicts among us do not significantly differ from the rest of us, as uncomfortable as it may make the rest of us to admit it. As a rule, a self-assessment along behavioral lines will give us a less admirable picture of ourselves than will one along psychological lines, at least if our self-assessment is comprehensive and does not concentrate exclusively on areas where our behavior matches our self-image.

Thus, the difference between addicts and nonaddicts lies neither in the tendency to choose self-assessments that favor the assessor, nor in the resulting general preference for using psychological rather than behavioral criteria in doing self-assessments. The difference lies, rather, in the tenacity with which addicts cling to the favorable self-assessments that are the fruits of the conjunction of those two factors.

Unlike the nonaddicted (or at least less severely addicted) among us, the severely addicted will cling so stubbornly to a positive self-*image* that they are unwilling to abandon it even when maintaining it is clearly against their own self-*interest*. They will cling to it even to the point of death, and in the face of even the most contradictory evidence. Something about addicts' pride will not let them give it up.

Addicts' Pride

We have to turn to an essay published twenty years ago and written by a psychologist rather than an academic philosopher to find one of the few places in the recent literature in which serious attention is given to some of the genuinely philosophical issues raised by addiction. In an essay that is still waiting for full appreciation in contemporary discussions of addiction, Gregory Bateson uses the language of cybernetics and systems theory to address what he calls the "logic" of alcoholism. Bateson himself puts double quotation marks around the term *logic* to call attention to the unusual way he is using it in the context of his discussion of alcoholism. What is at issue is the logic of something altogether illogical, by the canons of Western formal logic as it has been formulated ever since Aristotle. It is a logic, a way of reasoning, that can no longer be grasped by the categories and principles of those traditions of formal philosophical logic at all.

The logic of the alcoholic, as Bateson captures it, is like the logic of paranoia. Both are cases of the reasoning of those whose reason has left them. What Bateson has in mind is precisely what we are addressing in this chapter, the sort of nonsensical sense that Saint-Exupéry's tippler makes. What Bateson calls the "logic" of alcoholism is what we would here call the alcoholic mind. And what Bateson has to say can easily be extended beyond the confines of alcoholism to apply to all addiction.

At the heart of the "logic" of alcoholism Bateson finds what he labels alcoholic "pride." Again, the quotation marks are Bateson's own, and he uses them around *pride* for the same reason he uses them around *logic*. The way the alcoholic thinks (or, we can add, going beyond the limitations Bateson himself observes, the way the addict in general does) presents a sort of inside-out, upside-down image of what ordinarily counts as logical thought. Just so does the way in which the alcoholic (the addict, in general) maintains a positive feeling about himself or herself provide an inverted, distorted mirror image of genuine or legitimate pride.

Legitimate pride is based upon accomplishment or achievement, taking those terms in a broad sense. In that sense they are not to be confused with success, at least as it is ordinarily understood. The sense of pride can very well be founded upon the knowledge that one has honestly done one's best even if one has failed (even if one comes in last, to finish the race at all can often be a tremendous accomplishment). One takes pride in what one has done or tried to do, been or tried to be, insofar as it is a reflection one's own character and not, for example, the outcome of purely external factors over which one has little or no control.

What Bateson identifies as alcoholic "pride," in contrast, "is not contextually structured around past achievement." It is not a pride in oneself on the basis of one's own past accomplishments. "The emphasis is not upon 'I succeeded,' but rather upon 'I can . . .' It is an obsessive acceptance of a challenge, a repudiation of the proposition 'I cannot.'"[8]

Such illegitimate pride will not allow one to admit any limitations. Accordingly, as Bateson points out, when alcoholics run up against situations that suggest such limitations, they are subjectively compelled to prove themselves by attempting to demonstrate their control. And the greater the failure of such attempts, the greater is the alcoholic's felt need to repeat the attempt. Thus, the relationship escalates, as Bateson says: the more trouble mounts from alcoholics' drinking, indicating that they cannot control their drinking behavior, the more insistent do they become that they can still "handle" it.

If it is left untouched by external factors, an escalating process of that sort will continue until it finally reaches a point beyond which no further escalation is possible. Then breakdown of the entire system occurs. That is not, as such, a negative outcome, however. Rather, the point of breakdown is a critical juncture: it is a point of danger, to be sure, but it is also a point of opportunity. Only through the breakdown of the escalating relationship is the ground cleared for the exploration of new, nonescalating possibilities.

In the case of the alcoholic, coming to this critical point of breakdown is what in AA is termed "hitting bottom." Individual drinkers "hit bottom" at different stages in their drinking careers. Thus, for one person, it may take no more than the first brush with the legal system for an alcohol-related offense to precipitate the crisis. For another person, however, it may take loss of job, family, home, car, and other possessions, and even being thrown out on the street, to reach crisis point. For yet a third, the point of crisis may not come even then, but "might be on the other side of death," as Bateson puts it.[9]

At any rate, once that point is reached (if it ever is), alcoholics are finally faced with a radical choice. As stated in *Alcoholics Anonymous*, spoken from the vantage point of alcoholics themselves, alcoholics now have only "two alternatives." The first is "to go on to the bitter end, blotting out the consciousness of [their] condition as best [they can]"—blotting it out, that is, through continued drinking. The second is (to continue with the AA way of speaking) "to accept spiritual help."[10]

That is, alcoholics who reach that crisis point are given, as one alternative, the possibility of what William James in *The Varieties of Religious Experience* (which was itself one of the sources for the AA formulation) calls a "conversion" experience. In the broad sense at issue for AA (even if not quite for James himself), the notion of conversion does not have to involve any specifically religious element. In *Alcoholics Anonymous*, whenever the phenomenon at issue is referred to in terms of "spiritual experience" and a "spiritual awakening," special care is taken to distinguish between the "spiritual" and the "religious." Indeed, even the term *spiritual* is sometimes dispensed with altogether, and the phenomenon is simply called a "personality change" or a "psychic change."

However it is labeled, what is involved is a thoroughgoing reorientation of thought and attitude, a sort of sea change at the level of the fundamental way in which one relates to the world, including oneself and others. It is a global restructuring of the typical, habitual response patterns of the individual, whether brought about suddenly (as the language of "conversion" and "spiritual awakening" might suggest) or as the culmination of a long process (as may come more easily to mind when the talk is of "personality changes," for example). It is the reconstruction of the addict's psyche, the reconstitution of the addict's mind.

Reconstituting the Addictive Mind

Circular reasoning, enabling perception, and perverse pride are the three main features of addictive thinking as we have considered it. The new thought patterns that must emerge for a "psychic change" to occur, permitting the addict to escape addiction, must break the hold of those three old ones. The old thought patterns trap the addict in addiction and draw tighter in response to any attempts at extrication on the addict's part, escalating their demands until and unless a point of critical breakdown arrives. If escape from addiction is to occur even then, new patterns of thought must still emerge. Those new patterns must be able to immunize the addict against the old ones by replacing them with ways of thinking that display opposite qualities.

What patterns of thought can immunize one against the sort of circular reasoning into which Saint-Exupéry's tippler falls? Against the distortions of attention and perception that lead addicts struggling to stay "clean and sober" into what Marlatt calls "abstinence violations"? Against the illegitimate sort of pride that locks addicts into a downward spiral of addiction? In short, what might be the outlines of the *non*addictive mind?

For everyone who takes addiction seriously, that is a crucial question. However, the attempt to answer it lies beyond the confines

PART II

THINKING ABOUT ADDICTION

ships, responsibilities, and encumbrances, since they have already been *spoken for*: they have already been claimed by the objects of their addictions.

Addiction in the modern sense is the state or condition of being bound to such a master. Thus, even in that modern sense addiction is still a form of enslavement. Through their own acts, without ever clearly intending to do so, addicts ad-dict themselves: they speak themselves over to the objects of their addictions by vows e-nunci-ated in their behavior, vows in which they pro-nounce themselves addicts by an-nouncing their subservience to their new masters and re-nouncing their own claims over their own lives.

But just what, in turn, is involved in being a slave?

At least one obvious thing involved in being a slave is loss of freedom or liberty. Slaves, however, are not merely divested of liberty in the sense that certain choices are taken away from them. Parents who restrict how far their children may wander from home are not enslaving their offspring, and the laws that govern the behavior of the citizens of a state or country restrict those citizens' liberty without reducing them to the status of slaves. To be enslaved, one must suffer a restriction not merely of such choices and actions, but of one's very being. That is, one must be deprived, not merely of this or that specific right or group of rights, but of the fundamental right of living as one chooses, within whatever legal, personal, or other limits are imposed by one's concrete situation.

That includes financial and economic limits, no matter how severe. That is, being a slave cannot simply be equated with being deprived of economic rights and opportunities. The destitute and economically disenfranchised are still not slaves, no matter how debilitating, oppressive, and dehumanizing their condition. To be made a slave, it is not enough that one have most or even all of one's possessions or property taken away, or even that one be denied the chance to provide for oneself. To be made a slave one must be deprived of the right to dispose as one sees fit, not of one's property, but of one's very self. The slave is not the person deprived *of* property. The slave is the person who has *become* property. Slaves have lost proprietary rights not over things, but over themselves.

In the case of addiction in the modern sense, there is no independent enslaving power. No court or legal proceeding, no other person or class subjects the addict to enslavement. Rather, through their own choices and actions, addicts enslave themselves. In most if not in all cases, they enslave themselves without ever consciously aiming to do so, and largely as the result of factors—genetic and environmental—beyond their control. Still, since it is only through their own choices and actions that addictive enslavement occurs, it remains a form of *self*-enslavement.

However, that the enslavement is in that sense self-induced does not change the fact that addiction truly is *enslavement*—not just the rampant pursuit of immediate gratification, for example. How one comes to be enslaved (forcibly through others or inadvertently through one's own actions with what is at most covert, misguided acquiescence) does not alter the fact that one has become a slave. Nor does it alter what we might call the existential content of enslavement: the loss of proprietorship over one's own life—the loss of "own-ership" of that life.

Physical Aspects of Addiction

Addiction, then, is a form of enslavement. It is an existential state or condition in which one's very life has ceased to be one's "own."

Human beings are creatures of possibility. It is their fundamental possibilities that define them: such possibilities as finding themselves, or losing themselves altogether; as being grasping, possessive, and clinging, or open, generous, and liberating; as withdrawing from fellowship, or welcoming it; as living fully, or barely living.

Addiction is one of those possibilities. It is a way in which we can *be*.

As we shall need to discuss, addiction is not some sort of property that some individuals come to have and others do not have. It is not some physical state or condition. Nor is it a psychological one. Nor is it a behavior.

Rather, addiction is a *state of being*, like being damned—or being in a "state of grace." The title of a popular recent book on addiction is *Addiction and Grace*.[1] That has it quite right. Addiction and grace are indeed on a par. Each is a fundamental state of being, as opposed to some mere property or feature.

Very frequently in the popular media, but also often within scholarly work itself, addiction is depicted as though it were no more than a physical condition of the most straightforward sort—

namely, a condition defined by the conjunction of two physical factors. Those two factors are "tolerance" and "withdrawal symptoms."

"Tolerance" for a drug is said to have developed when larger doses are required to bring about the same effects that used to come from smaller doses. For example, the person who used to be able to calm his or her anxieties by taking one tranquilizer but who now has to take two or three to get the same effect has developed tolerance.

"Withdrawal symptoms" are distressful physical reactions that occur when drug usage is discontinued for enough time to allow residues from previous usage to begin leaving the body. Such reactions can conveniently be subdivided into two classes. The first is "stress reaction," which can range anywhere from mild irritability to convulsions and even, on rare occasions, death. The second is "backlash" or "rebound," which is the emergence, when the effect of the drug wears off, of the affect opposite to that originally induced by the drug. An example would be the onset of depression as the initially elation-inducing effects of cocaine begin to wear off.

Despite the popular image of addiction, however, the conjunction of tolerance and withdrawal symptoms does not define addiction. The conjunction of tolerance and withdrawal symptoms is neither necessary nor sufficient for addiction, even if we limit our discussion to drug addiction (we defer a discussion of whether one can also be addicted to processes for the next chapter).

Those who are addicted to drugs do not necessarily show both symptoms. Indeed, some addicts display neither.

The occurrence of withdrawal symptoms in cases of addiction is, in fact, quite variable. Studies have shown that the severity of such symptoms, sometimes even whether they occur at all, is largely a function of the interplay of what sociologists call "set and setting." This is even true for heroin withdrawal, which frequently counts in the public mind as the worst form of withdrawal sickness. For example, heroin addicts coming off heroin in a jail setting and having a mind-set toward withdrawal that leads them to expect discomfort and difficulty tend to experience more of these symptoms, with greater severity. For them, withdrawal from heroin addiction can be the shaking, sweating, jerking, arduous ordeal so often depicted in the media. On the other hand, addicts can be taken off heroin in a supportive hospital setting within a general hospital population that includes other addicts who have successfully withdrawn from heroin, and where an expectation of little or no withdrawal discomfort is conveyed. In this kind of setting suggesting such a mind-set, addicts' withdrawal symptoms tend to be less severe.

What is true of heroin addicts is also true of alcoholics; withdrawal from alcohol in cases of acute alcoholism is perhaps the most physically dangerous of all forms of withdrawal. Here again, whether withdrawal symptoms occur and, if they do, how severe they will be, seems to depend at least as much on "set and setting" as it does on such factors as the quantity and duration of alcohol ingestion over the alcoholic's drinking career. Indeed, sometimes the same patient will show withdrawal symptoms during one episode of detoxification, but fail to show such symptoms during a later detoxification. "But it is unsafe to base a diagnosis on an inconsistent symptom which ... can sometimes appear and on a later occasion fail to appear in the same patients," as Mark Keller, former director of the Rutgers Center for Alcohol Studies, points out.[2]

We find similar difficulties when we turn to tolerance, the other factor that is often taken to define addiction. In the first place, in many cases we often speak of addiction to a drug, even though there is no evidence that the use of the drug at issue produces physical tolerance.

In general, the evidence is clear that physical tolerance does develop at least with regard to what is termed *negative reinforcement.* However, it has not yet been conclusively demonstrated in the case of what is called *positive reinforcement.*[3]

Often misunderstood and confused with what is termed *punishment* or *aversive conditioning*, negative reinforcement occurs when some behavior is "rewarded" by the lessening of some unpleasant or painful affect. For example, if taking morphine alleviates physical pain, then the behavior of taking morphine is said to have been negatively reinforced. In contrast, positive reinforcement occurs when some behavior is rewarded with an increase of pleasant or desirable affect. An example would be a drinker experiencing a sense of euphoria after drinking alcohol.

The uncertain evidence for the development of tolerance to drugs

that predominantly involve positive as opposed to negative reinforcement for usage has not, however, stopped us from extending
the notion of addiction to cover the compulsive use of such drugs.
Cocaine, for example, is a drug of this type. Whereas cocaine used
to be regarded as nonaddictive, it is currently widely regarded as
highly addictive. That is especially true for the concentrated form
of cocaine colloquially known as "crack," the addictive potential
of which is sometimes exaggerated to hysterical proportions in the
popular media.

Furthermore, even if we confine our attention to drugs that bring
negative reinforcement for usage and have been proven to produce
tolerance (for example, morphine taken for the alleviation of pain),
it is at least highly questionable whether the usage of such drugs
must be in sufficient quantity over sufficient time to engender tolerance, in order for the drug usage to deserve classification as addiction. For example, imagine some "closet" drug user who carefully
confines his or her daily consumption to amounts significantly below the threshold that would be required in order to produce tolerance, but whose entire day is organized around that consumption
as the focus of daily life. Many, if not most, of us would have no
qualms in describing such an individual as addicted to drugs, even
though tolerance is not present. Once again, it would be wholly
arbitrary to declare such a person free of addiction just because
tolerance is not present.

At any rate, whether it is confined to negative reinforcement or
also extends to positive reinforcement, tolerance usually takes time
to develop. To become tolerant to the effects of a drug or drug
equivalent, the individual must repeat the drug taking or equivalent
behavior a number of times.

The same thing applies to withdrawal symptoms, to bring them
back into the picture too. The system shows withdrawal symptoms
only after a sufficient number of doses have been taken, if it shows
them at all. The body's chemistry must be given enough time and
dosage to adjust itself to the presence of the drug before the deple-
tion of that drug from the body will cause such symptoms.

Thus, the usual development of either tolerance or withdrawal
symptoms presupposes that a history of drug usage is already present. This is surely what William Burroughs had in mind when he

wrote concerning narcotics addiction, "It takes at least three months' shooting twice a day to get any habit at all."[4]

But Burroughs seems to have made the mistaken inference that the reverse is therefore also true: that three months' (or however many months') shooting twice a day will give one a "habit"—will result, that is, in addiction. "You don't decide to be an addict," he writes, correctly enough, as we noted in an earlier chapter. But then he continues, "One morning you wake up sick and you're an addict."[5] That remark makes it sound as if addiction is some purely physical condition that one unintentionally develops by repeating a certain behavior.

But just what is the behavior at issue, after all? As Burroughs has said, it is "at least three months' shooting twice a day." However, a person who shoots heroin or some other narcotic twice a day for three months without any medical reason for doing so is hardly a run-of-the-mill case. Why in the world, we might well ask, would someone inject a narcotic so often for so long a time unless that person was *already* an addict? Most of us would surely feel no great hesitation in calling such a person an addict.

Furthermore, suppose that one morning one does wake up sick. Even if one has been using drugs twice a day for the last three months, it does not follow that one will see any connection between one's drug usage and one's sickness. As Burroughs observed later in *Junky*: "I have talked to many addicts and they all say they were surprised when they discovered they actually had the first habit. Many of them attributed their symptoms [such as waking up sick one morning] to some other cause."[6]

Burroughs' point that the connection between the sickness and the drug usage is not obvious and immediate should be retained. Reservations apply to the rest of what he says, however. There is a self-serving potential for addicts to claim that their addictions came to them as a surprise. That same potential, in fact, lies in the very use of the term *habit* as a synonym for *addiction*. In the final analysis, there is nothing "habitual" about injecting oneself with narcotics twice a day over a prolonged period.

Something that has become habitual is something one has learned to do without thinking about it. That is the role of habit: to allow us to do things without having to bother to think about doing them, or about what we are doing while we do them. Thus, for example, after we struggle long enough with them, the movements and bodily adjustments involved in riding a bicycle or in swimming become habitual to us, so that when we climb on a bike or jump into a swimming pool we don't have to think about what we are supposed to do; we just do it.

That description does not, however, fit the case of someone injecting himself or herself with heroin twice a day. On the contrary, as Burroughs himself again attests in numerous passages, addicts quite consciously invest the whole activity of their drug taking with significance. They tend to ritualize it, sometimes giving even the most trivial surrounding circumstances the status of inviolable rites. Once again, set and setting play a major role.

In fact, treating tolerance and withdrawal symptoms as definitive of addiction involves a confusion of cause and effect. As Avram Goldstein, a neuroscientist who specializes in the study of addiction, argues, tolerance and withdrawal symptoms are common *results* of addiction, rather than components of addiction itself.[7]

Thus, neither tolerance nor withdrawal symptoms, let alone the conjunction of the two, turns out to be necessary for addiction. Nor is the conjunction of those two factors sufficient; that is, even when both are present, addiction may not be.

The best example is also a common one. Hospital patients who are given morphine or other narcotics for relief from pain can develop tolerance and can show withdrawal symptoms once the administration of the drug is discontinued. Nevertheless, they rarely become addicted. Most have no difficulty getting off the drug and are often grateful to be able to do so. In sum, then, tolerance and withdrawal symptoms are neither necessary nor sufficient for addiction.

As a final remark concerning these common physical accompaniments of addiction, it is worth noting that it is precisely because tolerance and withdrawal symptoms are at best uncertain accompaniments to addiction that many researchers have tried to distinguish between supposedly purely "physical" addictive dependency and "psychological" dependency. That terminology has, in fact, gained wide acceptance. However, only if we accept the idea of some purely physical state of dependency or addiction would there be any need to distinguish between that state and other similar but supposedly purely psychological states. As we have noted, such a purely physical addictive dependency cannot be established. Accordingly, the distinction between the two supposed kinds of dependency boils down, at most, to no more than the distinction between a dependency in which tolerance and withdrawal symptoms occur, and a dependency in which they do not occur, as Mark Keller has remarked.[8] That is, it is not really a distinction between two kinds of dependency at all, but rather between dependency in general and dependency that is symptomatically accompanied by other factors. The terminology of "physical" and "psychological" dependency has unfortunately become so common that an attempt to eliminate it would probably prove futile, but at least we can resist the tendency to import into that verbal distinction anything more than what has just been said.

The Externalization of Addiction

There is an underlying idea behind the popular notion that addiction is a purely physical condition. It is the idea that it is drugs themselves, through their actions on the body's chemistry (whether through slow accretion over a prolonged period of regular usage or through potent effects at first contact, as some current depictions of addiction to "crack" cocaine suggest), that "cause" addiction.

That idea has something attractive about it for drug addicts themselves, since it offers a convenient rationalization for their continued drug usage ("I can't help myself; drugs have got me"). But it is also convenient for those of us who do not fit the stereotype of the drug addict and who, furthermore, do not think of ourselves as addicts.

For the self-styled nonaddicts among us, the idea that it is the drug or its equivalent that accounts for addiction allows us to continue overlooking the presence of addiction and addictive tendencies in our own lives. If it is the drug or drug equivalent that causes addiction, then all we have to do is avoid the drug—or perhaps do no more than avoid regular, long-term usage ("three months' shooting twice a day," for instance)—to avoid addiction itself.

This idea that it is drugs themselves, or their equivalents, that cause addiction is a modern version of what, in the Middle Ages, might have taken the form of the *demonization* of addiction. That is, by externalizing the forces at work in the formation of addiction, attributing addiction to the properties of drugs themselves, we accomplish much the same thing as was once accomplished by attributing compulsive behaviors to the actions of evil spirits. Based on fear, such externalizations are common enough and easy enough to understand. By externalizing what we perceive as threatening within ourselves, we attempt to isolate ourselves from it and, even more importantly, to convince ourselves that it does not affect us in our innermost selves—to convince ourselves, instead, that we continue to be in full control of our own behavior.

The externalization of addiction that would make of it an inevitable result of sufficiently prolonged and sufficiently regular drug usage cannot, however, withstand criticism. The mechanisms of tolerance and withdrawal syndrome attributed to the effects of such usage would not explain addiction, even if they were granted universal occurrence among addicts (which, as we have seen, is far from the case). As shown by the example of hospital patients who gladly and rapidly come off medication and have no trouble remaining off it, even if tolerance has developed and even when withdrawal symptoms occur, being an addict is not a matter of having those two symptoms. Rather, being an addict is a matter that involves how one *relates* to such things as tolerance and withdrawal symptoms, if they do occur. Whether we are addicts or not is a matter of the *meaning* we attribute to such symptoms, the *significance* we discern in them.

For example, what makes Joe an alcoholic while Fred remains a social drinker is not how much alcohol either consumes, where they consume it, or even whether they get in trouble when they do consume it. What makes Joe an alcoholic is that, for him, alcohol has come to play a certain sort of role in his life.

Behavior and Addiction

Any attempt to define addiction as a purely physical condition overlooks that crucial point, but so do attempts to define addiction solely in terms of *behavior*. Thus, for example, the pharmacologist Jerome Jaffe defines drug addiction as "a behavioral pattern of drug use, characterized by overwhelming involvement with the use of a drug (compulsive use), the securing of its supply, and a high tendency to relapse after withdrawal."[9] Avram Goldstein (whose insistence that tolerance and withdrawal symptoms should be regarded as effects of addiction rather than as its causes or part of its definition we have already mentioned) cites Jaffe's definition with approval. Goldstein thinks that Jaffe offers a good reply to the World Health Organization's "dogmatic proscribing of the term 'addiction' as supposedly imprecise." He says that the various alternative terms WHO and others have proposed to replace *addiction* "seem to miss the point," whereas Jaffe's definition "brings the problem into good focus." That focus, he then writes, is that drug addiction "is a behavior, and it concerns the compulsive use of a drug."[10]

What neither Jaffe nor Goldstein appears to recognize, however, is that the notion of "compulsive use," so crucial to Jaffe's definition, is not itself any merely *behavioral* notion. There is no single set of "behaviors" that differentiates compulsive use of a drug from noncompulsive use. Compulsive drug use is not simply a matter of frequency or amount of usage, nor of where and when the drug is taken, for example. It is rather a matter, as Jaffe's definition puts it, of "overwhelming involvement" with the drug—overwhelming involvement with using it, securing its supply, associating with others who use it, and so forth. It is a matter, once again, of the meaning or significance (an "overwhelming" one, for the addict) with which one invests the drug. It is a matter of the place in one's life one gives to one's dealings ("involvement") with it.

To help reinforce that recognition, it is important to realize that the notion of addiction functions in our thought less as something that itself requires explanation, and more as something that explains something else.

A woman takes drugs intravenously twice a day over a period of time. The doses she needs today to attain the desired effect are significantly larger than they were when she started using the drug. Whenever she is forced to go without the drug for any length of time, she shows signs of stress and experiences a "backlash" reaction.

Why does this woman take drugs in such a way? Because she is a terminally ill cancer patient on medication for her pain.

A man also takes the same drugs intravenously twice a day for the same period of time. The doses he needs today to attain the desired effect are also significantly larger than they were when he started using the drug. Whenever he is forced to go without the drug for any length of time, he also shows signs of stress and experiences a "backlash" reaction.

Why does this man take drugs in such a way? Because he is an addict.

If we account for the man's drug taking by saying that he is an addict, we are giving a very different *kind* of account than when we say of the woman who takes similar drugs in a similar way that she does so for medical reasons. In effect, by saying that the man is an addict, we are denying that *reasons* are there for his drug taking at all—at least reasons in the sense that we would say the cancer patient has reasons for taking drugs.

Taking drugs because one is an addict is not like taking them for any specific purpose. The addict is by definition the person who takes drugs *for the sake of taking drugs*, rather than for the sake of some other desired end. For the cancer patient, the drugs are a mere means toward something else, namely, the alleviation of pain. In contrast, for the addict, drug taking has ceased to be a means toward something else; it has become an end in itself.

"I have learned the junk equation," writes Burroughs. "Junk is not, like alcohol or weed, a means to an increased enjoyment of life."[11]

To the casual drug user, drugs are just means to increased enjoyment. The same point is made about nonalcoholic drinkers in *Alcoholics Anonymous*: "For most normal folks, drinking means conviviality, companionship and colorful imagination. It means release from care, boredom and worry. It is joyous intimacy with friends and a feeling that life is good."[12]

Here, the end is an increase of positive satisfaction (positive reinforcement), rather than the lessening of pain, as for the cancer patient (negative reinforcement). What is common in both cases, however, is that the drug user relates to the drug as no more than a means to an end.

That is no longer true for the addict.

Most addicts "just drifted" into initial usage, to borrow another of Burroughs' self-descriptions. They did not begin with any self-conscious attempt to avoid pain or other negative affect. "You become a narcotics addict because you do not have strong motivations in any other direction," writes Burroughs.[13] Nor, once they have become addicted, can addicts' continued drug usage be explained simply in terms of the avoidance of negative affect, as already discussed. Finally, addicts do not use drugs just to get "high"—just for the "kick." Again, what may be true of the casual drug user is no longer true of the addict. As Burroughs pointedly puts it: "Junk is not a kick. It is a way of life."[14]

Thus, both *having cancer* and *being addicted* can count as explanations for the same behavior, but they do not both explain in the same sense. The fact of having cancer gives a reason for the behavior; it establishes a relationship between the behavior and some end for which the behavior serves as a means. The kind of explanation given is one that fits neatly into the categories of instrumental rationality. However, the fact of being addicted "explains" drug-taking behavior in a wholly different sense: by *removing* the behavior from the entire context of instrumental rationality and thereby removing the need (even the possibility) for explaining that behavior in terms of instrumental reasons. The addict no longer needs any "reason" to take drugs, since taking drugs has quite literally become the addict's very way of life.

·4·

Delimiting the Scope of Addiction: "Substance Addiction" and "Process Addiction"

Some individuals compulsively seek to gratify their sexual desires. Sometimes they will pursue such gratification even to the point of breaking up their families, damaging their careers, and harming themselves physically. Nor is it only rapists, child molesters, and other criminals who do such things. Among the ranks of those involved in compulsive behaviors are also doctors, lawyers, teachers, priests, secretaries, bank presidents, stockbrokers, housewives, and househusbands. To all appearances normal in other regards, these men and women cannot seem to control their sexual appetites, no matter how hard they try or how dire are the consequences of their failing to control themselves.

Their behavior with respect to sex is "as absurd and incomprehensible . . . as that of an individual with a passion, say, for jaywalking," to borrow an example originally used in a different context.

He enjoys himself for a few years in spite of friendly warnings. Up to this point you would label him as a foolish chap having queer ideas of fun. Luck then deserts him and he is slightly injured several times in succession. You would expect him, if he were normal, to cut it out. Presently he is hit again and this time has a fractured skull. Within a week after leaving the hospital a fast-moving trolley car breaks his arm. He tells you that he has decided to stop jay-walking for good, but in a few years he breaks both legs.

On through the years this conduct continues, accompanied by his continual promises to be careful or to keep off the streets altogether. Finally, he can no longer work, his wife gets a divorce and he is held up to ridicule. He tries every known means to get the jay-walking idea out of his head. He shuts himself up in an asylum, hoping to mend his ways. But the day he comes out he races in front of a fire engine, which breaks his back. Such a man would be crazy, wouldn't he?[1]

It is revealing that the example of the jaywalker comes from *Alcoholics Anonymous.* The compulsive jaywalker is given as an analogy for the alcoholic. But the analogy could just as easily be turned around, to show the many similarities between the jaywalker and the alcoholic. On the strength of that analogy, it is not unreasonable to suggest that we extend the notion of addiction, which already covers the case of the alcoholic, to cover the case of the jaywalker as well.

Of course, the example of the jaywalker is imaginary. It is a fictional exaggeration not meant to depict any actual individual or type. Nevertheless, the components involved in the behavior of the fictional, exaggerated jaywalker are anything but imaginary.

The mere activity of jaywalking is not of itself "absurd and incomprehensible." Rather, what makes the imaginary jaywalker's behavior absurd and incomprehensible are the lengths to which he is willing to go to pursue his chosen activity. And even if compulsive jaywalking is not a common occurrence, many other activities are pursued compulsively by significant portions of the population. As with jaywalking, most of these activities are perfectly comprehensible in their own right. But for each of them there are individuals who, as in the case of the imaginary jaywalker, cross over the line in their behavior—the line between the comprehensible and incomprehensible, between what, no matter how unusual it may be, remains acceptable and what has become altogether unacceptable.

So can one cross over the line in one's sexual behavior, to return to our initial example. The case of someone who has crossed over the line in sexual behavior is then functionally identical to the case of the imaginary jaywalker. Accordingly, it makes just as much sense to extend the notion of addiction to cover such sexual compulsivity as it would to extend it to cover such compulsive jaywalking.

That is precisely what many counselors and researchers have done. Beginning in the 1970s and coming into prominence in the 1980s, there has been an increasing tendency to treat such compulsive sexual behavior as a form of addiction. Patterning themselves on AA, groups of "Sex and Love Addicts Anonymous" have sprung up around the country. As that very name already indicates, the notion of addiction has been broadened to cover not only "sex addicts" but also "love addicts."

In turn, various subcategories of "love addiction" have been introduced, with some of the classification systems becoming quite elaborate. Thus, some authors argue that a variety of distinguishable forms of addiction is involved. The range goes from such relatively narrow divisions as "romance addiction" to the far more spacious "relationship addiction."

The latter has also been further split into two broad subdivisions. In the first, one is addicted to one particular relationship, so that one finds oneself unable to function whenever that one relationship (to one's spouse, for instance) begins to unravel. In the second, one is addicted to relationships in general, so that one feels the need always to be in *some* relationship, though with whom doesn't so much matter.[2]

What is more, the idea of addiction has, in fact, already been applied to a wide variety of altogether different sorts of behavior, beyond sex and interpersonal relationships—activities that really are more like our borrowed example of jaywalking. For instance, some researchers (as well as some of the persons they have researched) believe it is possible to become addicted to television. In addition, many experts as well as laypersons hold that one can become addicted to exercise, either in general or, more commonly, in one specific form, such as jogging or bicycling. Then, too, compulsive overeating can and has been treated as an addiction; and

Overeaters Anonymous has for quite a while been a well-established offshoot of Alcoholics Anonymous.

The Existential Equation of Addiction

To be addicted to something is to enter into such a relationship with it that one feels that things are fundamentally all right only when one is cultivating that relationship—but in which one does feel things *are* fundamentally all right whenever one is cultivating it, regardless of what else might be going on. If one is an addict, then no matter what else is happening to one, however disastrous, at bottom everything still feels all right—everything feels as if it is as it should be—so long as one can continue practicing one's addiction.

What the addict has been trained to do, in effect, is to *identify* "everything being all right" with practicing the given addiction. Whenever addicts are practicing their addictions, then by definition they feel "all right."

In contrast, whenever addicts are *not* practicing their addictions, it feels to them as if something is wrong. They feel "restless, irritable, and discontented," without ever being able to put a name to just what it is that is making them that way. In some way that they cannot further specify, things just feel out of joint to them.

It is not accidental that that feeling vanishes the moment addicts once again actively take up their addictions. For an addict *not* to "use" *is* a situation in which something is "not right"; after all, what addicts are "supposed" to do is to pursue their addictions.

Addicts have learned to identify themselves with their addictions, an identification that provides the connecting thread running throughout the entire fabric of their daily lives. When they are not practicing their addictions, that fabric starts to unravel. Only by returning to his or her addiction can the addict sew the fabric of his or her life back up again.

For example, while they are drinking, alcoholics will sometimes report that they feel fine, when all the physical and behavioral evidence says the contrary. That does not mean, however, that those self-reports are to be dismissed as false or delusional. Rather, precisely what alcoholics have learned is an experiential equation in which to feel all right *is* to drink, and to drink *is* to feel all right. Furthermore, that equation proves itself anew every time the alcoholic does drink, even if the world comes down around his or her ears when that happens.

Anyone who has ever been addicted to something has learned that same equation. The variables just change to fit the addiction, so that what existentially defines feeling "all right" for one person will be alcohol, for another it will be heroin, and for a third it will be picking someone up in a bar and going to bed with him or her, or watching reruns of "Gilligan's Island."

We now give this matter a closer look.

Expectancies and Addiction

One of the first serious psychological theories developed to account for alcohol consumption involved what came to be known as the "tension reduction hypothesis."[3] This hypothesis originally consisted of a single thesis, which was that drinking alcohol reduced tension. Later, a second thesis was added, which was that people drank alcohol *in order to* reduce tension (after all, even if drinking alcohol does reduce tension, that may be only a pleasant side benefit, rather than the main reason people drink it). To put the two together: people drink alcohol because it reduces tension.

Difficulties uncovered by subsequent research (such as the demonstration of the biphasic effect of alcohol consumption, discussed later in this chapter) have necessitated major revisions in the tension reduction hypothesis, if not its complete abandonment. One of the more interesting developments has been the emergence of "expectancy theory."[4] Basically, expectancy theory modifies the tension reduction hypothesis by changing the claim that people drink alcohol because it reduces tension to the claim that they drink it because they *think* it reduces tension. They drink alcohol because they *expect* it to reduce tension, even if it "actually" doesn't, as measured physiologically (by such factors as blood pressure and heart rate) or behaviorally (by such factors as fistfights, shouting matches, knifings, shootings, and eye gougings).

Despite what appears to be clear evidence to the contrary, many cling with persistent stubbornness to the expectancy that drinking alcohol will reduce tension—that drinking has a "relaxing" effect.

On the surface, such a rigidly maintained expectancy seems bizarre, given the contrary physiological and behavioral evidence. However, in the case of alcoholics, as distinct from the general drinking population, there is really nothing bizarre about it, as we can see once we recognize the role that the "existential equation" just discussed plays in addiction.

There is a religious peace that "passes understanding," a peace that is supposed to come from surrender to God (to speak within the Christian tradition, for example). Such peace passes understanding, because it is there even in the worst of times and the greatest catastrophes. It endures even intense grief and loss. In the midst of a sea of troubles, tossed between waves of pain and anguish, one's soul at its core remains serene, thanks to such peace.

There is, however, at least one perversely clever copy of that transcendent peace of God. It is this copy that addicts find by practicing their addictions.

Like the religious person experiencing the peace of God in the midst of the worst calamities, alcoholics maintain an underlying sense of everything being all right, even when they are raging with emotions and their life is a shambles, just so long as they can keep on drinking. In the same way, regardless of what their pulse rate, therapist, or checkbook balance may say, cocaine addicts have that sense of peace when they are using cocaine, and sex addicts feel it whenever they indulge their sexual obsessions. The same goes for other addicts practicing their addictions.

Thus, in a crucially important sense, an addict's expectation that practicing the addiction will alleviate his or her distress is well founded, rather than being something clung to despite the evidence. That is one major reason why addiction is so difficult to break. The addictive equation confirms itself every time the addict gives in to the addiction, and each confirmation just etches the equation that much deeper in the addict's mind. As the authors of *Alcoholics Anonymous* knew (and as they taught Gregory Bateson, for one), the only hope of breaking an addiction lies in a complete "psychic change." As is sometimes said in meetings of AA and its many offshoots, addicts don't have to change anything to recover from addiction, they just have to change everything.

The Objects of Our Addictions

Objects of addiction are like objects of affection. There is no end to the things about another person that might first strike me as attractive, leading me on to approach the other person. But that other person doesn't become "the object of my affections" until and unless I pass beyond what motivates such an initial approach, to devote myself and my attentions to the other person in a way that is irreducible to my attraction to whatever motivated that approach in the first place. Whatever so attracted me initially, that attractive feature did no more than issue me an invitation to such devotion.

If I do accept that invitation—if I go on and fall in love—then I will progressively discover more and more things that are attractive in my beloved. More and more features, mannerisms, gestures, and aspects of the other person will delight me, giving me more and more motive for my devotion. It is my very infatuation that makes all those details so appealing, of course.

In the same way, such things as the mood changes that I experience when I drink alcohol or inject myself with heroin may, if I find myself attracted by them, invite me to become addicted (recall my friend's one and only experience with heroin, which appealed to him so much it warned him off heroin for good). However, making an invitation is not the same thing as forcing an acceptance; what the mood changes invite me to do goes as much beyond enjoying those mood changes themselves as falling in love goes beyond enjoying the attractive features of one's companion. But once I have accepted the invitation—once I have become addicted—all I have to do to experience even more inviting features of the object of my addiction is to pursue the addiction, just as I have only to pursue the object of my affections to discover more and more attractions in someone with whom I am in love.

Objects of addiction also resemble objects of affection in that neither has to be an "object." Most objects of affection are persons, not things; while addiction to a thing—namely, to some substance, such as alcohol or heroin—is one of the most common forms of addiction, it is not the only one.

What counts in addiction is that one relate to something, whether a substance, a process, a relationship, or whatever, in such a way that one experiences oneself as unable to do without it. What counts is only that one learn the existential equation of addiction for that "object." If that is how I relate to heroin, then I am a junky. If I relate to alcohol that way, I am an alcoholic. But I can also relate to another person that way, in which case I am addicted to that person; or else I can relate that way to being in relationships of certain types with other people, so that I am a "relationship addict"; and so on.

In general, anything to which I can imagine relating myself in the way at issue is a potential object of addiction for me, even relationships themselves.

Once we clearly recognize the need to define addiction existentially, as discussed in the previous chapter, it should come as no surprise to us that there can be "process addictions" just as easily as there can be "substance addictions." It should not even come as a surprise if it were to turn out that for a number of addicts their "primary addiction" is to addiction itself—being addicted to being addicted. (If we keep in mind the *tempting* quality of addiction we discussed in the first chapter, we can see that something like an addiction to addiction plays a role in *all* addiction: addiction itself, as we emphasized there, is tempting; it has many attractive features.)

It is the failure to recognize the necessity to define addiction existentially (as "a way of life," to speak with William S. Burroughs) that above all accounts for reservations against extending the notion of addiction, extending it, for example, beyond cases in which the body develops tolerance to some mood-altering substance and shows withdrawal symptoms when it is deprived of that substance. Once we truly see addiction for what it is—a way of *being*—the grounds for such reservations vanish.

Nor is it only "metaphorically" that we can speak of addiction to processes. It is interesting, in that regard, to remember what we saw about the original meaning of the term *addiction* in Roman law, where it meant being delivered over to some master by formal pronouncement of a court. Given that original meaning, if there is a metaphor involved anywhere, it occurs in the application of the term *addiction* to cover cases such as alcoholism or the compulsive use of heroin.

The Role of Substances in Substance Addictions

When asked about extending the notion of addiction to cover compulsive sexual behaviors, one psychologist responded: "It's not an addiction. There's no substance involved. You can use it as a metaphor, but its oversimplifying a complex phenomenon, and that could be dangerous."[5]

Such a comment reflects the fact that psychiatrists and psychologists traditionally tended to restrict the use of the term *addiction* to cases in which some substance was involved. The criterion they used for diagnosing addiction was physical dependency on such a substance (with physical dependency itself defined in the old way as the conjunction of tolerance for the substance and withdrawal symptoms when deprived of it). Accordingly, if any substance could not be shown to produce tolerance and withdrawal symptoms in controlled laboratory experimentation, they refused to consider that substance addictive.

However, emerging difficulties with that definition of dependency (such as those discussed in the preceding chapter), coupled with the increasingly widespread application, even within professional psychiatric and psychological circles, of the notion of addiction to a far broader class of disorders, led to an eventual revision of diagnostic criteria. Thus, in the current edition of the *Diagnostic and Statistical Manual* of the American Psychiatric Association, the diagnostic definition of addiction has been broadened accordingly.[6] Now, the basic diagnostic criterion for addiction requires no more than that there be compulsive behavior pursued for relief from experiential discomfort or distress. The compulsiveness of the behavior, in turn, can be recognized by the fact that the person involved continues to practice it even when it has negative consequences for his or her physical, psychological, or social life.

Notice how the new diagnostic definition no longer specifically ties the idea of addiction to any substance. Any number of behaviors can be compulsively pursued for relief from distress, and only relatively few of them, such as drinking alcohol or using drugs, involve introducing a foreign substance into the body.

In the case of addictions that do involve such a foreign substance, just what role does the substance actually play, however? The answer to that question is far from clear.

The standard, traditional answer is that once the foreign substance (the alcohol or heroin or other drug) is introduced into the body, it has an effect upon the body's chemistry that is sufficient to alter the mood of the person taking it. Supposedly, it is this mood alteration that the person seeks to induce by taking the drug. The alteration may be no more than the lessening or elimination of the feeling of distress from which, by the diagnostic criterion already mentioned, the drug user is trying to escape. Or it may involve substituting a positive affect for such a negative one—the pursuit of a "kick." Often, both motives could be involved (that is, it might often be that taking drugs is both negatively and positively reinforced, to use an alternative way of putting the same point). In any case, what would be at issue is the mood alteration itself, which would be the end or goal to be attained by taking the drug.

In line with such reasoning, some of those who defend extending the idea of addiction beyond "substance addiction" to "process addiction" have argued that the processes in question have the power to bring about the same mood-altering changes in brain chemistry as do the substances to which one can become addicted. For example, sexual arousal may produce a mood-altering effect. If it does, that could be what the sex addict becomes "hooked" on, just as (by the standard idea under discussion) the drug addict or alcoholic becomes hooked on the mood-altering effects of the drug or of alcohol.

Studies might eventually show that, at least for some persons, the activity of watching television altered their brain chemistry in a way analogous to that in which alcohol or narcotics alter brain chemistry. If so, that would seem to count strongly in favor of the hypothesis that "television addiction" can actually occur.

Similarly, eating may induce such brain changes in compulsive overeaters, "jogger's high" may be an actual chemical change produced in the jogger's brain by running, and so on. In principle, it can be theorized that for each process in which someone, somewhere, sometime has compulsively engaged (as well as for some imaginable but as yet uninstantiated compulsive behaviors), that process has the same sort of mood-altering effect on those who do compulsively pursue it.

Addiction and Mood Alteration

However, that entire approach is misconceived. It is only a lingering positivistic prejudice—a prejudice that whatever can't be measured can't be real—that leads defenders of the idea of "process addiction" to postulate such analogies between the bodily effects of engaging in certain processes and the bodily effects of taking addictive drugs

There is a long-standing inclination in Western thought to identify reality as such with physical reality. What cannot be demonstrated to exist at the purely physical level is often treated as no more than an illusion or a convenient fiction. Thus, for example, we of the West have a tendency to treat psychosomatic illnesses as though they were "less real" than illnesses of a purely physical sort.

Evidence has been growing, however, that the acquisition and development of even supposedly purely physical illnesses can be strongly influenced by psychological and emotional factors. At the same time, such developments as the emergence of effective drug therapies for depression and other emotional-psychological maladies, coupled with the demonstration of the physical bases of diseases such as asthma, heretofore often regarded as predominantly psychosomatic, have also helped to change our thinking about the connection between the physical and the mental. Thus, although it is still far from eliminated, the prejudice in question has recently been greatly weakened.

Even if no evidence could be found to support the contention that sexual arousal, eating, jogging, or the like, had the capacity to alter the brain chemistry of some individuals similarly to heroin and other addictive drugs, it would not at all follow that there are no sex addicts, food addicts, or exercise addicts. Nor would it in any way follow that the application of the term *addiction* to such cases would be metaphorical, unless we continue to cling to the sort of positivistic prejudice we have just been discussing.

In fact, to be addictive, neither a substance nor a process needs to alter moods at all. In the preceding chapter we discussed Avram Goldstein's point that tolerance and withdrawal symptoms are not causes of addiction, but are only its frequent effects. In exactly the same way, mood alteration is not so much the cause of addiction as it is one of its effects.

To be fair, positive alterations in mood do have a role to play in the formation of addiction. But that is not because positive mood alteration as such is what initially tempts every addict into addiction. For some addicts the alterations of mood directly induced by taking some drug or engaging in some behavior are no doubt part of what attracts them to the drug or the behavior in the first place. However, it is by no means necessary that every addict fit that type.

Not many smokers begin their careers as smokers by experiencing a feeling of relief when they first inhale cigarette smoke (which is usually by one's teens). Instead, most choke and cough. They have to *learn* to enjoy smoking. Even beyond the coughing and gagging, they must learn to experience the disoriented sensation that comes from inhaling cigarette smoke as pleasurable. They have to learn to relax into that sensation, rather than fight it, which is the initial reaction of most first-time smokers.

Nor can positive mood alterations alone explain the emergence of addiction even among those addicts in whom it did play an important role. Presumably, it is not only those who go on to become addicted who experience the given mood alteration from the drugs or behaviors at issue. Others who take the same drug or engage in the same behavior would also, it seems safe to assume, experience similar effects. What needs to be explained is precisely why some persons become "hooked" on the drugs or behaviors while others with equal exposure do not.

Differences in brain chemistry surely play an important role. For example, it may be that the brain reactions of those who develop addictions to specific substances or processes differ in important ways from the brain reactions of those who do not. There is some evidence to support that contention. Nevertheless, no serious researchers are willing to ascribe addiction to such a cause alone, since then everyone with the brain reactions in question would inevitably become addicted upon exposure to the drug or behavior involved, whereas others would be free of all risk of developing addiction. At most, the evidence suggests that a significant proportion of the addicted population may have some such differentiating characteristics, indicating that there is more than a merely accidental connection; but that connection, whatever it eventually turns out to be, is nothing like a necessary or sufficient condition for addiction.

The evidence concerning mood alterations induced by the use of substances that are all but universally regarded as highly addictive is by no means all of a piece. For example, research has shown that the effect of alcohol on mood is *biphasic*.[7] It is only in small doses and for a short period immediately after it is consumed that alcohol produces a positive affect—a sense of relaxation and mild euphoria. In larger doses or measured over a longer time after ingestion, however, alcohol produces an exactly opposite effect, one of agitation and depression.

But the average quantities and periods of alcohol consumption for alcoholics are far greater than those involved for the first, positive phase. What is more, anyone who has ever spent any time in a bar knows that alcohol, at least when it is consumed in such a setting by those whose minds are set on consuming it there, does not soothe and calm those who drink much of it. Instead, it increases their belligerence and aggressiveness (let alone the noise level).

To summarize, positive mood alterations do not play a necessary causative role in the formation of all addictions, nor does everyone who experiences such mood alterations become addicted to what induces them. The contention that in order to be addictive, substances or behaviors must be capable of producing such alterations cannot be supported. Accordingly, to show that there can be addiction to certain processes as well as to certain substances does not require demonstrating that those processes induce such alterations in those who become addicted to them. As Stanton Peele, one of the first to extend the notion of addiction to relationships, has argued, addiction is not a matter of isolated sensations, but rather of the total experience in which the addictive behavior takes place.[8]

·5·

Classifying Addiction:
Disease, Disorder,
or Misconduct

In recent years there has been a great deal of debate about whether addiction is a disease. But that very way of asking the question—asking, "Is addiction a disease?"—puts up an obstacle to seeing what is at issue in deciding whether to categorize addiction as a disease or in some other way. To ask whether addiction "is" a disease makes it sound as if what is at issue is a simple factual matter.

The question, "Is addiction a disease?", looks the same as, "Is Paris the capital of France?", or, "Is water two parts hydrogen and one part oxygen?" Those questions are unambiguous, and the answers to them are clear and straightforward.

However, the question about classifying addiction as a disease is a very different kind of question. It is important to be clear about just what is involved in disagreements about the wisdom of that classification before we attempt to takes sides: We need to consider the real nature of the issue before we enter the debate about it.

The Nature of the Disagreement

In that debate, reference is often made to "the disease concept of addiction." One of the first points that needs to be made is that there is no such thing as *the* disease concept of addiction. That is, there is no single, universally accepted concept that is always meant when addiction is called a disease. Current discussions of the classification of addiction as a disease reflect a diversity of understanding of both of the key notions, addiction and disease. The result is that, instead of there being any single concept involved, there are a variety of similar but distinct "disease concepts" of addiction.

In much if not most of the literature no clear concept is articulated at all. Instead, a variety of disparate, sometimes even conflicting ideas are typically lumped together in a loose fashion, and then trotted out as needed for ad hoc purposes. That is as true for the opponents of classifying addiction as a disease as for the proponents.

Thus, it is necessary to attend carefully to what precisely is meant when a given author in a given context says that addiction "is" or "is not" a disease. Not only do different authors frequently mean quite different things when they talk of the idea that addiction is a disease, but so does the same author sometimes take that idea in one way, sometimes in another, without necessarily acknowledging (or even seeming to be aware of) the shift in meaning.

When the various remarks of the various parties to the dispute are taken in context, it turns out that in at least one sense there is generally far less difference between those who call addiction a disease, on the one hand, and those who insist it is not a disease, on the other, than the rhetoric of either side acknowledges. That is in the sense that all the parties are often in essential agreement about the basic *facts* of the case (namely, the basic facts about addiction). However, in another sense—an equally if not more important one—the difference between the two sides is a great one.

It is like the proverbial dispute about whether the glass with some water in it is half full or half empty. The two parties to the dispute do not disagree about the amount of water in the glass or about the amount of empty space. Their disagreement is really not about the glass and the water at all. Rather, it is about the attitude to be adopted towards the water and the glass—and, beyond that, toward things in general.

To say that the glass is half full, rather than half empty, is to highlight certain aspects of the situation at the expense of other aspects—namely, those very aspects that are highlighted by saying that it is half empty, at the identical but reverse expense of playing down the first set of aspects. In consequence, each way of speaking has its own focus, and its own suggestion of the attitudinal response that would be appropriate. Saying that the glass is half full calls attention to how much water is still left in the glass, and invites gratitude for it. Saying that it is half empty calls attention to how much water is already gone, and invites sadness at the loss.

In the same way, to call addiction a disease highlights certain things about addiction that are not highlighted by calling it something else. Accordingly, to be clear about whether we should call addiction a disease or not, what we really need to be clear about is what features of addiction we should highlight. Should we highlight those features that calling addiction a disease highlights, or should we highlight others?

In turn, decisions about which aspects of a phenomenon should be highlighted most should not be made in the abstract. They are best made in the concrete, as a response to the factors involved in the actual situation in which a decision is needed. Nor, once made, do such decisions have to be maintained at all costs. Instead, as the situation changes, we may need to reverse them, and then even perhaps reverse the reversal as the situation changes further.

For example, if my goal is to get home from work as rapidly as possible, then most of the time my best bet might be to take a certain route home. However, if a stretch of that route is under construction, it may better for me to take a different route. Then, when the construction is completed, it would probably be wise to go back to the original way of getting home. Thus, the quickest way home may vary from one day to the next, and it would be foolish of me to think that there was only one "right" way to go.

In the contemporary debates about addiction and disease, it often appears as if we had to choose between *always* calling addiction a disease, and *never* doing so. Once again, however, that is based on the illusion that the question of whether addiction is a disease or not is a simple factual question such as "Were dinosaurs cold-blooded?"

Which is correct, to regard the glass as half full or to regard it as half empty? The question is a bad one, since it presupposes that one of the two ways of taking the situation is always going to be the right way to take it. In fact, however, there are times when it is better to take the situation the one way, and times when it is better to take it the other.

Is addiction a disease? Well, there are times when it is helpful to look at addiction that way, and times when it is not helpful.

As Opposed to What?

Whether we call addiction a disease or refuse to do so is a matter of perception and attitude, just as whether we call the glass half empty or half full. But the example of the water glass gives us two nicely fleshed out opposites: empty, as opposed to full; full, as opposed to empty. There is no such simple "opposite" to disease, however, unless it be the condition of full health, and certainly no one would seriously maintain that addiction is equivalent to that. So when thinking about the question "Is addiction a disease?" we also need to ask ourselves "As opposed to what?"

In terms of the history of attitudes toward addiction, the most important answer to that last question is "willful misconduct." It was precisely as a reaction against the view of addiction as willful misconduct that the disease view was first developed, and it is against that same alternative that it is still most commonly defended.

A line that sometimes makes the rounds at AA meetings is that recovering alcoholics are, to give one version, "sick people trying to get well," as opposed to "bad people trying to get good." Well, before the disease view of addiction began to catch on, and still today where it has not taken hold, the common way of perceiving alcoholics and other addicts was precisely as "bad people"—people who intentionally engaged in practices they knew to be wrong. The sort of drinking alcoholics did was regarded as "sinful" or "immoral," for example.

The truth of the matter is probably that among the class of addicts as a whole—at least without regard to the distinction between those who are "in recovery" and those who are not—there are probably about as many bad or immoral people as there are within the general population. It is probably all the same, in that regard, whether we are dealing with addicts, cancer patients, AIDS sufferers, or BMW owners. If nothing else, the spread of the disease view of addiction has greatly helped to overcome the illusion that addicts as a group are significantly different from other people when it comes to such matters of ethics and morality. Very good people can have very severe addictions, just as they can have arthritis or a taste for raw oysters; and very bad people can also have all three.

Interestingly, when we confine our attention to addicts "in recovery"—addicts, that is, who are actively struggling to overcome their addictions—the picture changes somewhat. Thoroughly "bad" people tend not to last very long in AA or other recovery programs based upon AA's Twelve Steps. That is because the Twelve Steps themselves are the embodiment of a fundamental, functioning ethics. To recover from addiction through the Twelve Steps requires an ongoing commitment to strive to live honestly, openly, and unselfishly, which is hardly an appealing idea for any "bad seeds" among addicts. Since virtually all modern addiction treatment (at least in the United States) is either based upon the AA model or at least involves a similar emphasis upon becoming responsible for oneself and one's behavior, the same can be said for addicts who enter and persist in recovery programs in general.

That key ethical component of the process of recovery from addiction engenders a paradox. The emergence and spread of the idea of "recovery" from addiction is inseparably tied to the shift from viewing addiction as willful misconduct to viewing it as illness or disease (the shift from viewing addicts as "bad people" to viewing them as "sick people"). Yet to recover from their "sickness," addicts must strive to be responsible, caring, ethical individuals— "good people."

However, the fact that overcoming addiction requires efforts to improve one's character does not necessarily mean that addiction should not be classified as a disease. What it does mean is something we have already emphasized before: that addiction is no merely physical condition. Thus, given the nature of "recovery" from addiction, if addiction is a disease, it is not a purely physical one. Addiction, as we have also emphasized, involves the whole person. So if it is an illness, then—to use the language of *Alcoholics Anonymous*—it is a spiritual and mental illness as well as a physical one.

According to the same source, the spiritual dimensions of addiction must even be put first. It is there that recovery must begin.[1] Insofar as that is so, we can agree with Gerald May, author of

Addiction and Grace, when he calls addiction our modern "sacred disease," a disease that leads us into the Spirit[2] (a notion to which we return in a later chapter).

Complementarity of Various Ways of Viewing Addiction

No serious contemporary critics of viewing addiction as a disease would have us simply return to the idea that it is willful misconduct. Instead, they suggest yet other ways of viewing addiction. The most viable suggestion is that we view addiction as a *behavior disorder.*

Seen as a behavior disorder rather than a disease, addiction becomes less a matter to be addressed by physicians, more a matter to be addressed by sociologists and social psychologists, while still remaining something for which condemnation and punishment are not necessarily appropriate. Seeing addiction as a behavior disorder also encourages research into the multiplicity of factors that play a part in addiction, and reinforces the impression that we must respond to addiction at the public level, rather than just at the private one. Especially because modern behavioral science emphasizes the social determinants of behavior, viewing addiction as a behavior disorder helps us to realize that addiction in modern society is everybody's business, not just a concern for others (for "those people," such as street junkies and drunks in the gutter).

Thus, when we consider whether addiction is a disease or not, we need to think not only in terms of the opposition between disease and willful misconduct but also in terms of the opposition between disease and behavior disorder. In regard to thinking about all such oppositions, George Vaillant, an expert on alcoholism, makes an excellent point. He draws an analogy between contemporary physics and contemporary research into alcoholism, an analogy that can easily be extended to cover the study of addiction as a whole.

In physics the so-called principle of complementarity allows scientists to treat light simultaneously both as a wave and as a stream of particles, without being forced to choose between the two and say that light "really" is only one or the other. "Just as light can consist of both waves and particles," Vaillant writes, "just so alcoholism . . . can simultaneously reflect both a conditioned habit and a disease; and the disease of alcoholism can be as well defined by a sociological model as by a medical model."[3]

AA members have learned to apply such a principle of complementarity as a matter of course. They shift easily from talking about alcoholism as a "potentially fatal disease" (a medical model of alcoholism), to talking about AA as a program for "learning how to live once you're done drinking" (in effect, a "social learning" model of recovery in which alcoholism appears as a behavior disorder), to talking about how the "selfishness and self-centeredness" they think is the root of their problem requires the practice of an ongoing "moral inventory" to maintain sobriety (a moral model).

That is itself a model of the complementary use of models. It does not betray inconsistency and confusion, but rather provides a genuine grounding in the experience of addiction. The example it provides helps us overcome the illusion that identifying something as a disease is like identifying Santa Fe as the capital of New Mexico—a simple matter of fact. It also helps us realize that we do not have to choose once and for all between calling addiction a disease and calling it a behavior disorder (or a moral failing, for that matter). We no more have to make such a choice than we have to choose once and for all between calling those with whom we have an intimate relationship lovers and calling them friends (or "significant others," for that matter). Sometimes one is appropriate, sometimes the other. We should avoid becoming addicted to either.

Applying the Medical Model
of Unitary Diseases to Addiction

Even which model of *disease* we should apply to addiction can vary. One major reason there is no such thing as "the" (namely, one and only one) disease concept of addiction, but rather a variety of different disease concepts, is that there is no one, single concept of disease itself. We can mean any number of very different things by that term.

The greatest debate has surrounded the application to addiction of one more or less specific medical model of disease. According to that model, to be a disease it is not enough to be a departure from health or a destructive, harmful condition or process. Instead, a disease has to be a unitary health-destructive process with (1) a specific cause, (2) a regular progression, and (3) characteristic symptoms.

Often, when someone talks about "the" disease concept of addiction, what turns out to be at issue is the application to addiction of that one medical model of disease—most especially the application of at least parts of that model to alcoholism by E. M. Jellinek, a physiologist and biostatistician who founded the Yale (later Rutgers) Center of Alcohol Studies and served as its first director. Jellinek's seminal book *The Disease Concept of Alcoholism* appeared in 1960. The model of alcoholism he articulated there attributed to alcoholism both a regular progression through distinct and sequential stages, and characteristic symptoms—two of the three criteria just mentioned. Jellinek was more hesitant about the third, specific causation. In fact, at one point he acknowledged "the fact that there is not one alcoholism but a whole variety."[4]

Jellinek's own discussion of the merits and demerits of calling alcoholism a disease is still well worth reading. For one thing, he is aware of some of the ambiguities involved, especially in common usage. "For the nonmedical man," he writes, to give one important illustration, "the word disease conjures up a vision of blood, rashes, emaciation, and generally a horrifying appearance." As Jellinek goes on to note, "That is not the case with the word illness, which in everyday language denotes something less frightening." Thus, he concludes, "In connection with alcoholism the term illness is more acceptable to the public than disease, of which they think rather in terms of the infectious diseases."[5]

It is interesting to note that Bill Wilson, co-founder of AA and author of *Alcoholics Anonymous*, consistently used the term *illness* rather than *disease* when talking about alcoholism.[6] It seems that Wilson himself did not want to call alcoholism a disease because there is no such thing as an alcoholism-carrying virus or microbe or the like. To that extent, Wilson would be an example of Jellinek's "nonmedical man" who thinks of disease solely "in terms of the infectious diseases."

What finally matters is not the choice of terms, *illness* or *disease*, but the actual nature of alcoholism and how closely it fits the unitary medical model in terms of the three features, specific causation, progressive development, and characteristic symptomatology. The same applies when we move from alcoholism to addiction in general. Therefore, we need to consider each of those three features in turn, inquiring into the extent to which addiction displays them, if it displays them at all.

What Causes Addiction?

As already mentioned, Jellinek denies that there is only "one alcoholism." He speaks instead of "varieties" and "species" of alcoholism. If that way of speaking is reasonable concerning alcoholism, it is even more reasonable concerning addiction in general.

Furthermore, even when we confine our attention to only one "variety" or "species" of addiction, to use Jellinek's terms, it may turn out that we are still not dealing with just "one thing." Rather, what is true of addiction as a whole may also be true of each of its parts. To borrow a well-known analogy from the twentieth-century philosopher Ludwig Wittgenstein, it is not only the rope as a whole that is made up of interlocking strands, but also the strands themselves that, in turn, are made up of interlocking threads (and the threads of interlocking fibers, for that matter). To a large extent, as it is with the rope, so it is with addiction.

To that same extent, then, it would seem that the question of what causes addiction would also be answered. Since addiction is no one thing, but a variety of different things, there would seem to be no one cause of addiction, but rather a variety of different causes. It might seem plausible, for example, to postulate a different cause for each variety of addiction. Insofar as each variety in turn is still not one single thing, but a variety of things, there might even be a multiplicity of causes for the same variety of addiction.

In general, that is more or less what research into addiction has shown. Today, the consensus is that there is no single identifiable cause or set of causes of addiction.[7] That is so for both psychological and sociological causes. The evidence shows that there is no distinctive "addictive personality," for example, and that addiction is not caused by any specific traumatic incident or by childhood problems.[8] Nor does poverty or any other sociological factor, either alone or conjoined with others, inevitably make anyone subject to that factor into an addict.[9]

As for possible *genetic* causes of addiction, the evidence is that genetic factors can certainly increase the risk of developing addiction, but by no means do they make it inevitable. That leaves only the idea we have already considered and rejected in the chapter on defining addiction—the idea that it is alcohol, drugs, or other objects of addiction that cause addiction by their physiological effects. We pointed out in that chapter that such an approach is ultimately insupportable, and that its popularity derives from a process of externalizing addiction, a modern version of demonization. In the case of alcoholism, for example, it is no more true that regular, recurrent heavy drinking inevitably results in alcoholism than it is that having alcoholic parents does so. To be sure, both factors increase the risk for developing alcoholism, but neither can plausibly be regarded as invariably causing it.

Thus, in the sense we have so far been discussing, the evidence shows no simple physical cause for addiction, any more than it shows any simple sociological or psychological causes. In that sense, there seems to be no one specific cause of addiction, making it appear that addiction fails to fulfill that criterion of the medical model for unitary diseases.

However, that is not the only possible sense of the idea of having a specific cause, just as infectious disease is not the only sense of the idea of disease. Especially if we keep in mind the root meaning of the term *disease*—namely, that of dis-ease: of discomfort or distress, the experience of disorder and suffering—then a sense in which addiction can be said to have but one cause, a cause we can clearly identify, begins to emerge.

As George Vaillant, whom we have previously mentioned, has written, "The point of using the term *disease* [in regard to alcoholism] is simply to underscore that once an individual has lost the capacity consistently to control how much and how often he drinks, then continued use of alcohol can be both a necessary and sufficient cause of the condition that we label alcoholism."[10] At first glance, that may sound like a version of the discarded idea just mentioned, that what causes alcoholism is sustained excessive alcohol consumption. There is a crucial difference, however. Vaillant's remark applies not to how an individual develops alcoholism in the first place, but to the continuation of the condition of alcoholism as a malady, once it is developed. What he is saying can be restated this way: Once someone has become an alcoholic, it can happen that all the individual has to do to continue suffering from that condition is to continue drinking, whereas the only thing that will bring recovery from that condition is to cease drinking.

Thus, properly understood, the import of Vaillant's remark is that there does remain a legitimate sense in which we *can* say that alcoholism has a specific identifiable cause, and, accordingly, fulfills that criterion for a unitary disease, medically speaking. That is the sense in which, as Vaillant puts it, continued consumption of alcohol can be taken as both the necessary and sufficient condition for alcoholics to continue suffering from "the condition that we label alcoholism"—from, that is, the literal dis-ease of alcoholism.

We can generalize to addiction as a whole: for any addiction, a necessary and sufficient condition for those who suffer from the addiction to continue suffering from it (to continue suffering from their dis-ease) can be to continue to "practice" the addiction at issue. In that sense, then, we can say of addiction in general that it fulfills the first of our three medical criteria for unitary diseases.

"A Progressive Illness"?

"We are convinced to a man that alcoholics of our type are in the grip of a progressive illness. Over any considerable period we get worse, never better."[11] That passage from *Alcoholics Anonymous* has become the classic statement of the idea that alcoholism is progressive.

The qualification, "of our type," is important. Better than forty years after the publication of *Alcoholics Anonymous*, George Vaillant made a similar point with a similar qualification:

> Whether alcoholism is viewed as a progressive disease depends very much on whether the spectrum of alcoholism is approached from the side of heavy drinking or from the side of clear alcohol dependence. . . . if one looks at those individuals whose alcoholism *has* been progressive (that is, relapsing alcohol-dependent individuals seen in alcohol clinics and emergency rooms), then alcoholism certainly appears to be progressive. In contrast, by following heavy alcohol *users* prospectively (say, individuals with a single alcohol related traffic violation), one finds that many such individuals may occasionally abuse alcohol without exhibiting progression. The most dramatic evidence for

alcoholism's being progressive was seen ... where the life course of 100 consecutive admissions to an alcohol detoxification unit were depicted for the next 8 years. At the end of that time span, only 24 patients were still abusing alcohol; almost all the rest had either died or become abstinent.[12]

As critics of the idea that alcoholism is progressive would be quick to point out, if we try to take such reflections as formal arguments, then they turn out to beg the question. Of course, the critics could note, if we confine our attention to individuals whose alcoholism *has* been progressive, then the resulting picture of alcoholism will show it to *be* progressive. As for the remark in *Alcoholics Anonymous*, the alcoholics of the "type" in question are precisely those whose histories are those of Vaillant's "relapsing alcohol-dependent individuals seen in alcohol clinics and emergency rooms." Since such circular proceedings are clearly illegitimate, critics could reject the contention that alcoholism is progressive as "unscientific."

However, such criticism would be unfounded.

When Bill Wilson and the other early AA members responsible for *Alcoholics Anonymous* say they are "convinced to a man" that alcoholism is progressive, we have to ask just what it is that convinces them. Is their claim an empirical generalization on the basis of their own limited experience, for example? If that were so, then the critics would indeed be right. If what Wilson and the others had done was review their separate stories with a eye to common features, which they then generalized to apply to all alcoholics of their type, then indeed the sample of alcoholics involved would have been far too narrow and selective to legitimate their claim. If their goal was to acquire new empirical knowledge about alcoholism by such a procedure on the basis of their own observations, then their procedure was completely unsound.

That, however, was not their goal. They did not proceed by way of generalization on the basis of empirical data collected in an endeavor to gain new knowledge about themselves as alcoholics and their condition of alcoholism. What they did, instead, was critically to reflect upon their own experience in an endeavor to arrive at an understanding of themselves and their condition. It was not any empirical generalization that served as the basis of their conviction that alcoholism is progressive. Rather, it was what they took to be an illuminating insight into the very nature of their alcoholism itself.

The idea of progressiveness allowed them to pull together and make sense out of their own experience, and the similar experiences of others like them. It was this experience of insight into alcoholism—of discovering an integrating way of looking at alcoholism, one that finally allowed them to discern meaningful patterns in their own histories as alcoholics—that convinced them, not some procedure of generalizing induction, and not any formal argument. And generations of subsequent AA members have confirmed the illuminating, integrating power of that insight as, sometimes suddenly and at first contact, sometimes slowly and against initial resistance, they have come, by identifying with the stories told by the AA members who have preceded them, to see signs of the "progressiveness" of alcoholism in their own "drinkalogues."

That is also why the conviction of such alcoholics that their alcoholism is progressive cannot be shaken by the criticism that empirical data do not support it. Because, unconsciously if not consciously, the alcoholics know that their conviction derives from other sources, they remain unmoved by any attacks along those lines.

The book *Alcoholics Anonymous* itself contains a number of stories, not only in the long "Personal Stories" section that follows the 164-page "basic text" but also in that basic text itself, in which the details of the drinking careers of the alcoholics involved show great exceptions to the fundamental progressive model to which Wilson and the others subscribed. But instead of treating these exceptions as though they invalidated the idea of the progressiveness of alcoholism, they treat them as variations from the progressive norm that are to be explained by the intervention of other factors. Far from being unscientific, that is a standard scientific procedure.

Thus, to give but one example, there is the story in Chapter 3 of *Alcoholics Anonymous* about the young man on the verge of a successful career in business who decides that he can't handle his liquor. Motivated by a strong desire for success in business, he therefore doesn't take a drink for the next twenty-five years. Then, after retiring from a successful career, he begins to drink again, only to end up "dead within four years."[13]

This story is especially interesting because it serves a double function. On the one hand, it demonstrates the idea that external factors, such as a strong motivation to succeed in business, can intervene in, and arrest, the progression of alcoholism, even for alcoholics of Bill Wilson's and the other AA members' "type." On the other hand, it simultaneously demonstrates the very idea of progression—in this case, an accelerated progression that takes only four years to go from the first drink (at least the first in twenty-five years) to the grave.

Characteristic Symptoms?

What Vaillant says about the question of progressiveness in alcoholism also applies to the question of characteristic symptoms of addiction in general: The further one goes along the spectrum of addiction, the more characteristic become the symptoms. The behaviors and patterns of occasional "users," for example, even those who get into legal or social trouble from "using," vary far more than do those of full-blown addicts. Such physical symptoms of addiction as cirrhosis of the liver in alcoholics follow the same curve, for obvious reasons, as does the incidence of personal, professional, and social-legal difficulties associated with "using."

Furthermore, our general conclusions about the idea that addiction is progressive can also be adapted to apply to the idea that there are characteristic symptoms of addiction. That is, the conviction that addiction involves such symptoms is finally a matter of having a certain insight into the nature of addiction.

That belongs to the very notion of a characteristic symptom, for that matter. Whether we regard a given symptom as characteristic or anomalous for a given condition depends on what we take to be definitive of that condition in the first place, just as whether we take a given gesture to be characteristic of a given person depends on what we take to be that person's character. The mere fact that some person makes a certain gesture repeatedly does not of itself make us regard that gesture as characteristic of that person. We may write it off to a nervous tic or some other such thing that we do not see as especially expressive of the distinctive personality of the individual involved. Being expressive of underlying personality is essential to what we regard as genuinely characteristic of the individual. In the same way, only if we take some symptom to be expressive of the underlying nature of addiction do we regard it as a *characteristic* symptom.

Addicts will always differ from each other in numerous ways, and there may well be no one symptom that most addicts have in common. Not every addict has employment problems because of his or her addiction, nor do all of them have broken marriages, and so forth. But that no more demolishes the claim that there are characteristic symptoms of addiction than the recognition that there are few textbook cases of the progression of addiction demolishes the claim that it is progressive. Once again, since such claims do not emerge from generalizations on empirical data, they cannot be overthrown by appeals to such data.

In addition, the two ideas—that addiction is progressive and that it has characteristic symptoms—are closely interconnected. The very notion of progression requires that there be regular stages in the development of a disease, and each stage itself needs characteristic symptoms by which it can be recognized and diagnosed. Conversely, symptoms themselves will always be characteristic of a given stage, and they will be counted as characteristic in the first place only if they are taken to be expressive of the progress of the disease at issue.

Thus, it stands with this third criterion for disease in the unitary medical sense as it did with the first two. The question of whether addiction fulfills those three criteria is no more a simple, straightforward, factual question than is the broader question to which it belongs, the question with which we began, of whether addiction is a disease at all: at every turn we come back to our water glass, either half full or half empty.

PART III

UNDERSTANDING ADDICTION

·6·

The Essence of Addiction

Using and "Thinking Using"

We have seen that addiction cannot be reduced to a physical condition or a psychological state. Instead, addiction must be defined existentially. Addiction is a fundamental state or condition of being. It is a way of taking up life as a whole and concretely living it out.

The addict takes up life and lives it out by centering everything around the given object of addiction, whether that be drugs, alcohol, sex, or any other substance or process. For the addict, as discussed in the first chapter, the addictive way of focusing everything through the lens of the addiction introduces a remarkable *clarity* into life as a whole. Once one has ad-dicted oneself to a substance or process—once one has spoken oneself over to it—then all of the troubling questions and problems of life are at once resolved. From then on, one no longer has to worry about what to "do with oneself," either at the moment or in the long run.

As for the first—moment-to-moment living—addiction has a way of filling up all of the addict's time. Let alcoholism again be the example. Even the worst alcoholic is not always drinking. There are always periods of sleeping, eating, and other daily and occasional activities besides the actual drinking that fill up the greatest part of any alcoholic's day. That continues to be true no matter how far we go along the continuum of alcoholism in the direction of chronic drunkenness. And the further along the continuum we go in the opposite direction, toward mere occasional overindulgence, the *less* time do alcoholics actually spend drinking alcohol.

Nevertheless, as members of Alcoholics Anonymous often remark, regardless of how much time they actually spent drinking, back in their drinking days, their concern with alcohol was pervasive. As they like to put it, even when they were not actually drinking, they were still always "thinking drinking." That is, they were planning how they were going to get their next drink, or looking forward to drinking after work, or perhaps just holding on until the time came when they could finally take a drink, meanwhile going through their daily routine in numb thoughtlessness.

To be "thinking drinking" does not necessarily mean to be consciously thinking *about* drinking. "Thinking drinking" includes such conscious, directed thinking about drinking, but is not limited to it. One way in which alcoholics can think drinking is by spending a lot of time imagining themselves in a bar, or entertaining themselves with thoughts of how they will be able to drink once their work or chores are over, or mentally making arrangements to procure more liquor, or actually thinking *about* drinking in some other way. But thinking drinking also includes simply orienting one's day around the times one does drink, anchoring the day there. In this way of relating to the day, one only truly comes alive when drinking time finally rolls around. For the rest of the day, one just puts oneself on "automatic pilot," in effect.

A popular automobile bumper sticker in ski country reads simply, "Think snow!" Avid skiers know what that means. It means to give oneself what we could call a "snow mind-set." To think snow is, as it were, to dedicate one's thoughts to snow, as one might dedicate a portion of one's income to charity. Skiers "thinking snow" are not always imagining snowy scenes or the like. They are adopting a mental stance that invites snow—comporting themselves as though snow is already on the way, just about to fall, maybe already falling, even if it is July and the temperature outside is hitting 100. Given that mental posture, devoted skiers will often do such things as hum "Winter Wonderland" or draw doodles of snowflakes. But they behave in such ways *because* they are "thinking snow." Thinking snow often and naturally manifests itself in thinking about snow, rather than the former being reducible to the latter.

To give another example, in his *Rule*, St. Benedict of Nursia, father of Western Christian monasticism, exhorts his monks perpetually to keep the fear of God before their eyes, that is, always to conduct themselves in the awareness of standing before God. As one twentieth-century Benedictine has written, what should first come to the lips and minds of good monks if asked what they are doing at any given moment is something along the lines of "serving God" or "going to God."[1]

Borrowing from the skiers among us, we could say that Benedictine monks are always supposed to "think God." They are supposed to think God at every moment, even when they are not thinking *about* God at all.

Insofar as they do always think God, it is certain that monks will also often think about him as well. In fact, if they do not frequently think about God, by way of praying, hearing, and reading what is for them his Word in the Bible, then they will no doubt soon stop thinking God, too. For that matter, in order first to become good monks who are always and everywhere thinking God, novices must precisely discipline themselves through regular prayer, scriptural reading, meditation upon such reading, and the like. Only through the practice of such disciplines of frequent and recurrent conscious "thinking about God" do monks become persons who continually "think God."

Thus, thinking God and thinking about him are clearly inseparable. The latter, thinking about God, is both a necessary means to the former, and an inescapable expression of it. Nevertheless, the distinction between the two thought processes is still important. Frequent thinking about God is for the sake of constantly thinking God, which, in turn, naturally manifests itself in thinking often about God.

The same is true of all lovers, not just lovers of skiing and lovers of God. When we are in love, we are "preoccupied" with thoughts of those we love. We think *of* them constantly, even though no lover can constantly think only *about* his or her beloved.

That is no less true of perverse forms of love than it is of genuine, healthy love. It is no less true, for example, of someone who loves drinking the way an alcoholic does, than it is of someone who loves God the way a Benedictine monk is supposed to love him.

No alcoholic is always drinking, but every alcoholic is always thinking drinking. The same applies to all addicts. No addict is always using (whether the "using" is taking drugs, acting out sexually, gorging on potato chips, or whatever), but every addict is always thinking using. It is for that reason that addiction can fill up every moment of the addict's day.

Addiction as Oblation

Not only does addiction fill up the addict's day, but it also fills up the addict's entire life. In that regard as well, the addict presents a perverse analogue to the monk. Once they have made their permanent vows, monks no longer have to concern themselves with such things as career choices. The question of what they are to do with their lives has been settled. By their formal vows they have dedicated their lives to God. All that remains after that is to live up to those vows. (Of course, that is no easy matter. Couples who have exchanged traditional marriage vows can attest to that. Those vows are no less "permanent," as vows, than are those that bind monks.)

As psychologist Stanton Peele puts it, to become addicts we must "give ourselves over to addiction."[2] In the first chapter, besides discussing how addiction clarifies life by reducing it to such dimensions as eyedroppersful of morphine solution or shotglasses full of rye, we also made the same point Peele does. We pointed out that, although addicts do not deliberately set out to become addicts, it is just as true that they do not become addicted *despite* themselves either. Addiction does not happen by mere chance. It does not occur by accident. Rather, it occurs in response to the temptation to become addicted—in response to the invitation to give oneself over, as Peele says, to addiction. Addicts are persons who have yielded to that temptation, accepted that invitation.

In St. Benedict's day and for a long while thereafter, it was the custom on occasion for families literally to give one of their children to a monastery. Sometimes that happened in fulfillment of an oath, made in exchange for a divinely granted petition. For example, a farmer might promise his next child to the local monastery if God had granted him a record harvest in answer to a heartfelt prayer. In other cases, it occured as an act of penance for some sin. Another class of cases was probably that of devout but impoverished parents who found themselves unable to feed another mouth, and who gave their child to the monastery as much for the child's own sake and for the sake of its siblings as for their own.

The children who were so given to the monastery were called "oblates," which comes from a Latin term (the past participle of *obfere*) meaning "to offer." Such children were offerings to God. Their parents made such offerings of their children in formal written documents of "oblation."

The institution of Benedictine oblation has undergone many changes during its long history. It still survives today, but in a form very different from what it was originally. Parents no longer give their offspring to monasteries—but those offspring, once grown, sometimes still give themselves. Modern oblates are women and men who do not become monks, but who nevertheless feel themselves strongly enough drawn toward Benedictine monasticism and its spirit that they choose formally to affiliate themselves with some monastery. Most of them remain active in the "world," pursuing secular careers. But in formal documents of oblation kept by the monasteries they have selected and that have agreed to accept them, these men and women pledge fidelity to those monasteries and promise to strive to live their own lives in the spirit (and, whenever reasonably possible, even by the letter) of St. Benedict's *Rule*.

Addicts are like such modern oblates. They offer themselves up to their chosen addictions just as surely as Benedictine oblates offer themselves up to God. Where the oblates make an offer of themselves to their monasteries and to the *Rule*, addicts give themselves over to their substances or processes of choice.

Addicts do not write up formal acts of oblation like Benedictine oblates, but that is primarily because the gods they serve do not require any; they don't need to. In that regard, the way addicts' gods accept their devotees is very different from the way the Benedictines' God accepts those who offer themselves to him, as we will discuss in the following section.

"Disownment" as the Essence of Addiction

It is surely, as both the Jewish and the Christian scriptures tell us, a terrible thing to fall into the hands of the living God. That is no doubt still true even when the falling is initiated by one's own voluntary leap, as it is in the case of the Benedictine oblate. It is also a terrible thing to fall into the hands of an addiction such as alcoholism, even when every drink one takes is by one's own choice. However, the two terrors are of very different sorts.

We no longer have the option of signing our children away to monks. However, if they act up too much or for too long we can still "disown" them, as we say. That is, we can write them out of our wills, deny them access to our property, refuse to speak to them, and do whatever else is necessary to divest them of the inheritance that would normally fall their way as our children.

In this case, where we speak of disowning our children, we use *disown* as an active, transitive verb: *We* disown *them*. Here, to disown means actively to dispossess another.

Many psychologists, psychiatrists, and counselors, especially Jungian ones, speak of "disowning" in a slightly different sense. They talk about the "disowned" parts of *ourselves*. Those are the parts or aspects of ourselves that, for one reason or another, we so wish we didn't have that we try to reject them. We try to be rid of them, to deny that they are really our "own." But since what we disown in this fashion truly is a part of us, we can push it away only at the price of turning ourselves into fragments of full-fledged people. If we are ever to become whole again, the reasoning at issue proceeds, we must learn how to integrate *all* of our parts, most pointedly including the disowned parts. Here, accordingly, to disown does not mean to dispossess another, but to deny a part of oneself—and to *be* dispossessed in the process.

In yet a third way of using the term, we can speak of "disowning" our responsibilities. By that we hardly mean that we are writing our responsibilities out of our wills. So the first sense of disowning is not at issue. What we mean is closer to the second sense of *disowning*, the one Jungian psychologists favor; but even that does not really capture what is at issue. Rather, to disown our responsibilities is to "wash our hands" of them, as Pilate in the Christian scriptures washes his hands of responsibility for the crucifixion of Jesus. It means to distance ourselves from them, to absolve ourselves from them. When we disown responsibility for some event, we deny any claims that might be made against us pertaining to that event. Here, to disown is neither to dispossess another nor to dispossess oneself, but to disavow something that might otherwise be attributed to one.

There is a common meaning element that unites the three senses of *disown*, despite the differences among them. That is the element of rejecting, discarding, or casting off, as one might discard an old set of clothes or cast off a cloak or a disguise. To disown one's child is to cast the child off. To disown parts of oneself is to cast them off. To disown one's responsibility for some event is to cast off all possible claims that might be made against one for the consequences of the event.

In its essence, addiction is a complex process of dis-own-ment at the level of that fundamental meaning element, of disownment as casting off. It involves movements of dispossessing, of being dispossessed, and of disavowing, all three. In turn, each of those three movements within addiction reinforces the other two; and the interaction of the three creates a vortex of disownment at the very heart of addiction. Left unchecked, addiction will eventually suck everyone it touches into that vortex, beginning with the addict, and then extending to family and friends, and then to ever more distant circles of contact, finally affecting the addict's society as a whole.

In accordance with its nature as an existential condition, however, addiction does not draw its victims into its vortex as though it were an externally imposed fate. Instead, addiction dis-owns by implicating its victims in their own victimization. That is precisely why it is so hard to break free from addiction.

As we put it in the first chapter, in dealing with the tempting quality of addiction, a great part of the power of addiction over addicts themselves comes from addicts wanting their addictions, even when they do not want to want them. By restating that same point in a slightly different form, we can begin to see the sense in which addiction dis-owns the addict, and how it does so. It will also become visible that here is one of the places that viewing addiction as a behavior disorder proves helpful (provided, at least, that we remember to treat that way of viewing addiction as a complement to viewing it as a disease, or even viewing it in terms of moral failings, rather than as the only acceptable perspective). If we do view addiction that way, we can apply what is called social learning theory to explain the paradox at issue. For ease of discussion, we again take the case of the alcoholic, as we have repeatedly done before.[3] As before, the results can easily be expanded beyond alcoholism to cover addiction in general.

Restricting attention to alcoholism, the paradox that needs to be accounted for can be clearly indicated this way: alcoholics both *do* and *do not* choose to drink. First, we consider the sense in which they do choose to drink. Then we turn to the sense in which they do not choose to drink.

As we remarked back in the first chapter, no one needs to hold alcoholics down and force liquor down their throats. Instead, alcoholics reach for their drinks with their own hands. Hence, at that level there would appear to be nothing involuntary about alcoholism. Alcoholics simply choose to drink on the occasions that they do drink. The problem at that level of analysis is just that they make that choice—the choice actually to drink—too often, and in inappropriate circumstances.

However, the involuntary nature of alcoholism does appear at the very next level of analysis. That is the level at which we ask *why* alcoholics make the choice to drink as often as they do make it.

As we have also already discussed, what is definitive of alcoholic as opposed to nonalcoholic drinking is that the former is noninstrumental drinking. That is, the alcoholic is someone who drinks for the very sake of drinking, rather than as a means to some other end. Viewed from a social learning perspective, that means that their underlying social conditioning has preprogrammed them, as it were, to choose to drink under a whole host of situations in which no clear, independent end is to be served by the drinking. In a nutshell, although alcoholics choose to drink on any given occasion when they do drink, it is still true that, at least on those occasions when their drinking is symptomatic of their alcoholism, *they do not choose so to choose.* That is, as alcoholics, they regularly make the choice to drink, but they did not ever choose to make that their regular choice.

All this deserves further reflection. Let us begin by taking an extreme case. It is not uncommon among alcoholics in recovery to encounter the idea that there may be some physical mechanism at work such that, for at least some alcoholics, the ingestion of any amount of alcohol sufficient to trigger that mechanism results in continued ingestion, wholly beyond the effect of mental set or social setting. In fact, the bulk of the evidence does not support that contention. Nevertheless, even if we do assume that we are dealing with such a mechanism, it still does not explain what (as the authors of *Alcoholics Anonymous* clearly showed they knew, when they wrote of being "without defense against the first drink") really needs explaining. What really needs to be explained is why alcoholics time after time pick up the first drink, the very one that will set off the supposed mechanism in question.

But that is just what viewing alcoholism in terms of behavior disorders and social learning theory allows us to explain. Viewing alcoholism from that perspective suggests that the best way to define the alcoholic is not as someone who habitually *drinks*, but as someone who habitually *chooses* to drink. What is involuntary is not the actual drinking as such. What is involuntary is the recurrence of the choice to drink.

Social learning theory correctly emphasizes that even alcoholic drinkers drink because they judge drinking to be the most desirable option in the given situation. On every occasion when drinking actually occurs, even alcoholic drinkers make a *choice*. It is a matter of a conscious decision at least to *begin* drinking. In that sense, their drinking is always the expression of rational deliberation, in the broad sense of that term, and not the inevitable result of some mechanical process entirely beyond their control.

To that extent, then, the drinking of the alcoholic does not differ from that of the social drinker. In both cases, drinking is a matter of conscious choice. That is not what makes the alcoholic an alcoholic, as opposed to a social drinker (or even a nonalcoholic "problem drinker").

What makes the alcoholic an alcoholic is not, therefore, that the alcoholic has no choice over drinking, as if alcoholics will inevitably drink even if, on the given occasion, they choose not to drink. If the drinking of alcoholics were involuntary in *that* sense, then the condition truly would be hopeless. Even the AA way could not work, since the fundamental strategy behind AA's estimable "one day at a time" approach requires that the alcoholic be able *by choice* to refrain from drinking at least for "today." (That is how it is put, for example, in the story of the third member of AA, the first to be brought into the fold by Bill Wilson and Bob Smith, AA's co-founders, after Dr. Bob attained sobriety. The way the root idea is presented there is that anybody, even the worst alcoholic, can refrain from drinking, if he or she so chooses, for "just twenty-four hours."[4])

So what makes the alcoholic an alcoholic, as opposed to a nonal-coholic drinker, is not that alcoholics have no choice at all, on certain occasions, over the onset of their drinking. On any given occasion when they actually do drink, alcoholic drinkers choose to drink no less than do nonalcoholic drinkers. Rather, what makes an alcoholic an alcoholic is, that that very choosing is no longer at the alcoholic's choice. That is, it is no longer a choice that is deter-mined by the alcoholic's rationally sovereign and free assessment of the situation in terms of possible means for achieving selected ends, as is true for the social drinker. Instead, for the alcoholic choosing to drink is determined by past social learning or condi-tioning.

For alcoholics, drinking will occur only when they choose to drink. But alcoholics *will* choose to drink far more often, and on far more occasions on which their drinking will have negative re-sults, than nonalcoholics. In effect, their *drinking* may be voluntary, but their *choosing* to drink has ceased to be so. Because of whatever underlying conditions (including genetic factors), the alcoholic has been taught to choose drinking in situation after situation in which, objectively considered, drinking has nothing to contribute to the alcoholic's interests and may even run contrary to them.

Alcoholics have learned a wrong lesson, in accordance with which, time after time, drinking will appear to them to be the best available option in the given situation, even when that turns out not at all to be the true case. Because it appears to them as the best option, they will, of course, choose it. But that choice itself has, in reality, ceased to be *their own*. It has ceased to be a choice which expresses their own control of their own lives, and mastery of the options (however limited or dire) those lives afford them.

Thus, alcoholism dis-owns alcoholics in a very radical sense. It literally disinherits alcoholics of the basic right to dispose of their own lives as they see fit. Alcoholics are no longer at their own disposal. Instead, they are at the disposal of the conditioning that distorts their perceptions in favor of drinking in situation after situation in which drinking is very far indeed from the best option available to them—"best" in the morally neutral but existentially fundamental sense of being most in accord with the underlying truth of *who they are*.

As noted in *Alcoholics Anonymous*, alcoholics are typically men and women "whose disposition while drinking resembles [their] normal nature but little." A man who is an alcoholic "may be one of the finest fellows in the world. Yet let him drink for a day and he frequently becomes disgustingly, and even dangerously anti-social."[5] The same thing also applies to women alcoholics.

For both men and women, if they are alcoholic, then the persons they become when drinking are often not "themselves" at all. Their own drinking histories give them clear evidence of this fact. Yet time after time these same men and women choose to drink again, with the same results. What accounts for such bizarre behavior? Why do alcoholics repeatedly make such a demonstrably mistaken choice?

The answer is that it is no longer the alcoholics *themselves* who are making that choice. It is their addiction choosing. And what the addiction chooses is to disinherit alcoholics of the right of disposal over their own lives and to deny them to themselves, and then to wash its hands of all responsibility, leaving alcoholics each to their own private hells.

Codependency and Addiction

Addiction progressively dis-owns addicts by robbing them of governance over their own choices. To the degree that they are thus divested of what we might call their own "share" in themselves (as we can own a "share" in a business), addicts are moved to invest themselves in their addictions. They come to hold shares in those addictions as such.

Addicts, however, are not the only ones who are given a share in their addictions. So are those with whom addicts share their lives—their so-called codependents.

By virtue of their dis-own-ment by their addictions, of being radically dispossessed of themselves by them, addicts have a *direct* interest or investment in their addiction. The alcoholic has a direct interest in finding excuses to drink, for example. The drug addict has a direct interest in procuring drugs and using them. The relationship addict has a direct interest in entering into a relationship or maintaining a current one. All of them have a direct, vested interest in "maintaining the supply."

Dispossessed of themselves by addiction, the only self left to addicts is addiction itself. To practice the addiction becomes more and more their exclusive preoccupation, as they become less and less themselves.

To the extent that other persons enter into any sort of relationship with addicts, those other persons are also drawn into the movement of addictive disownment. Insofar as they have a relationship with an addict, they necessarily have a relationship with addiction, since addiction has become the very "self" of the addict as such. The more severe the addiction, the greater is this identification of the addict with the addiction itself, and the more the other person in a relationship with the addict is also involuntarily drawn into relationship with the addiction.

Whereas the addict has a direct interest in maintaining the addiction, the other person in a relationship with an addict comes to have an *indirect* interest in maintaining it. Having lost themselves to their addictions, addicts must now maintain their own addictions in order to maintain the only selves left to them. Thus, maintaining the addiction literally becomes maintaining themselves. However, insofar as another person enters into a relationship with an addict, that other person also takes on an interest in maintaining the addict's addiction as the necessary means for maintaining the *relationship*. If the relationship is to continue, then the addict's addiction must also continue, since there has come to be an existential identification of the one with the other. Hence, because the other person has a direct interest in maintaining the relationship, that other person comes to have an indirect (though unconscious) interest in maintaining the addiction.

The addict's *direct* interest in maintaining the addiction makes the addict dependent on the object of the addiction. (The alcoholic is dependent on alcohol, the drug addict on drugs, and so forth.) If another person enters into a relationship with the addict, then that other person's *indirect* interest makes him or her *also* dependent on the object of the addiction. He or she has become dependent on it *along with* (and through) the addict. He or she has become a "codependent."

Through their codependency, codependents are also dis-owned by addiction right along with the addicts with whom the codependents have entered into a relationship. Time after time addicts choose, against their deepest, truest selves, to "use," thereby maintaining the very addiction that holds them in thrall, dis-owning them of those very deepest selves. Just so do codependents also choose time after time, and against their own deepest, truest selves, the very courses of action that are best suited, not to break addicts' thralldom to addiction but to maintain it and even strengthen it. That is, to use the terminology that has emerged in the contemporary discussions of the phenomenon at issue, time after time codependents choose to "enable" the addicts with whom they have entered into relationships.

The classic example is that of the spouse of the alcoholic who makes excuses for the alcoholic's conduct that protect the alcoholic from the consequences of that conduct, consequences that might confront the alcoholic with the fact of his or her alcoholism. The codependent spouse makes calls to the alcoholic's employer, lying about the alcoholic being sick at home, when the only sickness is really nothing but the hangover from the preceding night's drinking. Or the codependent pays the bills the alcoholic has run up during a blackout. Or the codependent accepts the alcoholic's assurances that "it will never happen again," letting the alcoholic come back home "just this one more time." In these and countless other ways, the codependent ends up protecting the alcoholic—and in the process protecting the supply of alcohol—helping to maintain the very addiction that keeps the relationship in turmoil.

By Love Dispossessed: Codependency, Addiction, and Enabling

The twentieth-century philosopher Martin Heidegger distinguishes between two different ways in which we can be loving or caring toward others.[6] In the first way, what we do is always to leap in *for* those we love. We do things for them, so that they don't have to do them for themselves. We protect them from things we think might harm them. We give them things we think are good for them. We stand up for them, and stand in for them. In short, we "take care" of them.

In the other way of loving or caring for others, we don't leap in *for* them, taking care of them. Instead, Heidegger says, we leap *ahead* of them—leap ahead in order to clear the way for them to do things on their own and take care of themselves.

Contemporary discussions of so-called codependency have provided us with a handy terminology for talking about the distinction Heidegger has in mind. One characteristic of codependency that is recurrently mentioned in the pertinent literature is the tendency toward "caretaking." By that is meant precisely what Heidegger captures as the first way of caring for others: leaping in for them. If we reserve the term *caretaking* for that first possibility, then we can call the second one (leaping ahead of others and clearing the way for them) "caregiving." That gives a nice terminological contrast between care*taking* and care*giving*.

What caretaking does is literally that—it *takes* cares *from* the care receivers toward whom it is directed. It removes cares from them, lifts their cares off their shoulders. When we tell someone that we will "take care of everything" pertaining to some matter, we are telling the other person that he or she does not need to worry about that matter any further, but can leave everything in our hands.

In general, any caretaking that goes beyond what is truly necessary tends to accomplish the very opposite to what it most truly intends to accomplish. At least that is so under the assumption that we are dealing with an expression of genuine love or caring for another person, as opposed, say, to a manipulative device to control the other for consciously selfish purposes.

As such an expression of genuine loving or caring, caretaking aims at the good and well-being of those who are its recipients, rather than at the selfish good of the caretakers themselves. That is its own deepest, most essential intention. However, unnecessary caretaking (leaping in for others and taking care of them when they really don't need it) deprives its recipients of the opportunity of learning how to care for themselves, creating a reliance on the caretaker where independence and self-reliance could otherwise develop. Those whose needs and wants are always being met by someone else are denied the chance to explore their own personal capacities to take care of themselves, and to reap the rewards that come from doing so—rewards in the form of self-esteem, a sense of security that comes with knowing that one is able to fend for oneself, and so on. Addicts come to depend on their caretakers for everything, without ever being allowed to discover their own real limits and abilities.

Of course, there are situations in which it is necessary and legitimate that we take care of others, providing them protection and the satisfaction of their needs. Those are precisely the situations in which there is a real incapacity on the part of care receivers to take care of themselves. Children, the ill, the permanently or temporarily incapacitated—all require others to take care of them to one degree or another, sometimes for mere survival, sometimes in order to have maximum opportunity to grow and flourish, or to recover from the very malady that may have robbed them of the capacity to care for themselves in the first place. At one time or another (if not always, to one degree or another) we all fall into such categories, so that we truly do need others to take care of us at least to some extent.

Nevertheless, even in such cases truly to love and care for others requires that we limit our caretaking of them to the real limits of what they cannot do for themselves. We need to let those for whom we care do as much as they can for themselves, or, where necessary, with our help, rather than trying to do everything for them. Otherwise, we rob them of sovereignty over their own lives by making them dependent on us—or creating the illusion that they are dependent, an illusion that is as effective as the real thing.

What is called "enabling" in the literature of codependency involves just such caretaking. However, it is absolutely crucial to understand the *kind* of caretaking that is at issue, and to be careful to restrict the usage of the term *enabling* to cases of that kind.

First, as we have already mentioned in passing, to be properly labeled "enabling," the caretaking at issue must be *genuinely loving or caring behavior*, as opposed to veiled manipulative behavior. The spouse of the alcoholic "enabling" the alcoholic's drinking to continue by making excuses for the latter's drink-related absences from work is not consciously and deliberately aiming at doing something that feeds the alcoholic's alcoholism. Far from it. The codependent spouse is doing the only thing he or she can see to do to try to *help* the alcoholic. The problem is one of ignorance, not malice.

To that extent, codependents have something in common with addicts themselves, who, as we have already discussed, habitually choose to "use," not out of malice but out of conditioned misperception of the options available to them in various, recurrent situations. In exactly the same way, codependents habitually choose courses of action that end up enabling the addicts in their lives. But they do so because they have *learned* to do so. They make the choices they make—the very ones that end up being "enabling"—because they honestly perceive them to be the best options available to them at the time, the best options precisely in terms of *caring* for the addicts involved. When they enable, codependents act out of love, not out of any desire to manipulate addicts to their (the codependents') own selfish ends. The love manifest in enabling behavior is no less genuine for missing its mark.

The second condition that must be fulfilled if caretaking is properly to be classified as enabling is probably easier to understand. It is the condition that the caretaking truly be *unnecessary*. For example, suppose an alcoholic falls while drunk and sustains a wound that is serious enough to require immediate medical attention. It is hardly "enabling" to drive the alcoholic to the emergency room of the local hospital. Indeed, it would be criminal not to do so.

Enabling, then, is a form of caretaking that is unnecessary, but nonmanipulative. Nevertheless, it shares with directly manipulative caretaking, as will all caretaking that is not really necessary, this trait: It is not truly in the best interest of those toward whom it is directed. As does manipulative caretaking, enabling robs its recipients of their independence.

Put paradoxically, enabling *dis*-ables. By doing so, it dispossesses addicts of themselves under the appearance of helping them. Enabling furthers the movement of dis-own-ment that is the essence of addiction itself. It belongs *to* addiction as part of that very movement.

In contrast to the care*taking* that is involved in enabling, care*giving* would refuse to take addicts' cares away from them. Caregiving, as the very name implies, does not take the cares off the shoulders of its recipients. Instead, caregiving *gives* its recipients their own cares. It literally helps care receivers to pick up their own burdens and hoist them on their own shoulders. By leaping ahead and clearing the way, caregiving makes it possible for the care receiver to assume his or her own proper, personal cares.

Enabling disables. So does any unnecessary caretaking. In contrast, caregiving makes possible. It empowers.

Enabling and the Dis-own-ment of the Enabler

So far, we have been considering enabling in terms of how it affects the addict—the enabled. However, it is just as revealing to shift focus and look at what enabling does to the codependent—the enabler.

Enabling dis-owns the enabler no less surely that it does the enabled. When they enable addicts with whom they have relationships, codependents substitute themselves for the addicts, doing for the addicts what they can and should do for themselves. But through that very substitution codependents end up sacrificing their own interests to what they perceive to be the interests of the addicts toward whom their caretaking is directed. As they become more and more exclusively concerned with taking care of the addicts in their lives, they become less and less able to care for themselves.

As we have seen, addicts' lives become so narrow that they can be measured in eyedroppersful of morphine solution or shots of whiskey. The same narrowing also occurs for codependent enablers of addicts. For codependents, everything in life reduces down to the endeavor to protect the addict from the immediately threatening consequences of the last drunk or its equivalent, coupled with the struggle to maintain the illusion that things will somehow, God knows how, "get better," if only those consequences can be avoided "just one more time."

In that way the codependent becomes locked into a hopeless, repetitious round of enabling that is no less a dis-own-ment of the codependent that addiction is of the addict. Such codependency shows the same experiential characteristics as does the addiction in relation to which it *is* codependency. For the codependent, codependency is no less experientially tempting, tranquilizing, disburdening, alienating, entangling, self-dissembling, and self-perpetuating than addiction itself is for the addict.

Thus, both addicts and codependents are dis-owned in the movement of addiction. Both cease to belong to themselves any longer. Instead, each is spoken over—the addict directly, and the codependent indirectly, "along with" the addict—to addiction.

The dis-own-ment of the codependent is so radical that the very love expressed by the codependent's enabling behavior is deprived of its inherent sense and nature. The "care" in the enabling caretaking is perverted into its very opposite. Having originally sprung from the genuine love and concern that the codependent has for the addict, enabling actions end up harming the addict by unintentionally helping to sustain the addiction. The codependent's attempt to show care for the addict by protecting the addict from the consequences of addiction is thereby transformed into protection for the addiction. It is forcibly drafted into service of the addiction for "securing the supply." The love and care at the heart of the codependent's relationship to the addict is literally de-natured, stripped if its own underlying, definitive intention. It is made no longer its "own," its proper self: It is "dis-owned."

Institutionalized Addiction and Addicted Institutions

It is not only spouses, lovers, relatives, and friends of addicts that the movement inherent to addiction forces, along with addicts themselves, into service, dis-own-ing each in turn. Employers, employees, colleagues, coworkers, and any other persons in continuing contact with the addict are also drawn into the vortex of addictive dis-own-ment. How strongly each is drawn varies directly with the closeness of the daily involvement with the addict, just as water draining from a bathtub goes faster the closer it is to the drain hole.

It belongs to the essence of addiction—belongs to dis-ownment—to institutionalize itself. For present purposes, an institution is nothing more than a fixed form into which a process of human interaction with oneself, others, and things has settled. The repetitivenenss necessary to all addiction, the repetitiveness of the need for the "fix" and all the ritual and preparation that accompanies it, means that addiction from the very beginning sets itself up in such fixed forms.

At the same time, by fostering codependency and enabling, addiction also tends, of its own nature, to establish institutions at the level of all the social structures to which the addict belongs. Those structures begin with the immediate family and stretch all the way out to include the entire society, up to the global level. They are institutions that function, beyond and against the will of any individuals within them, to protect addiction and further the general movement of dis-own-ment.

Thus, it is not only at the level of individual codependents that certain recurrent, enduring patterns of individual behavior and interaction with others (which pattern are already "institutions" in the broad sense) tend, on their own and apart from the intentions of the individual codependents themselves, to foster addiction (to "enable"). It is also at the level of families, neighborhoods, cities, states, and society in general that certain recurrent, enduring patterns of social behavior and interaction ("institutions" in the narrower sense) tend to foster addiction, apart from any deliberate institutional or social policy toward that end.[7]

For example, leniency towards drunken drivers on the part of enforcement officers and the courts tends to enable drunken driving, rather than to lessen it through mercy, as is surely a common intention among those displaying such leniency. The questionable value of such practices has come more and more to public attention in recent years, thanks in large part to the efforts of Mothers Against Drunk Driving (MADD) and similar groups.

The effects of such enabling institutions, which foster addiction indirectly and unintentionally, should be kept distinct from those of public policies that foster addiction in far more direct ways, for the benefit of special interests. So, for example, to say that cigarette advertising aimed at encouraging teenagers to begin smoking "enables" nicotine addiction would be highly objectionable. Enabling is one thing, "pushing" is another. So is institutional protection for special interests that promote addiction.

In contrast to such intentionally addiction-fostering institutions, the formation of *enabling* social institutions, properly so called, is a moment in the movement of dis-own-ment that belongs to the very essence of addiction itself. Here, talk of "blame" is out of place. To blame those who act on behalf of such institutions makes no more sense than to blame individual codependents for their acts of enabling. In both cases, codependent "interest" in addiction remains indirect and unsought; and remedy to the harms engendered by enabling, as by addiction as such, must proceed through learning and education, regardless of the institutional level at which the enabling occurs. Ignorance, not viciousness, is at the root of enabling, at whatever level. However, no such mitigating ignorance is in play when it comes to those "pushers" and their supporters, again at whatever level of analysis, who have a direct, consciously self-serving interest in addiction, and who deliberately foster it.

Addiction dis-owns not only addicts and the individuals who share those addicts' lives, but also the institutions it forces into codependent service. Those institutions, in common with individual codependents, come to have an indirect, undesired interest in maintaining the very addictions that victimize them, through the addicts along with whom they are brought into addictive dis-own-ment. This addictive dependency at the heart of codependency is no less powerful, for all its indirectness, than is the direct dependency at the heart of addiction as such.

Codependent, enabling institutions are themselves caught inextricably in the dis-own-ment of addiction. Engendered by addiction, they share in its nature. They are themselves "addicted" in the broadest sense. In institutionalizing itself, addiction also creates such addicted institutions. In them, addiction fulfills its essence, making addictive dis-own-ment a pervasive, inescapable milieu. Wherever one looks, everything now belongs to addiction. Whoever "one" may be, whether the solitary individual or the larger community, nothing remains one's own.

The Dis-Owned Self

We have been discussing how one can suffer dis-own-ment through addiction even if one is not, in the narrow sense, an addict oneself. One can accept the temptation of addiction either through becoming directly addicted oneself, or through becoming a codependent. In either case, once one has accepted addiction's illusory offer, the dis-own-ment is the same. From then on, struggle as one might against the movement of addiction, one can no longer escape its grip. The very efforts to free oneself only entangle one more inextricably.

Although he never uses the word *addiction*, let alone the term *dis-own-ment*, St. Paul, the Christian apostle to the gentiles, gave a vivid description of the experience of the addictively dis-owned self nearly two thousand years ago. As Paul expresses it in a famous passage, the experience of the dis-owned self is that of a loss of ownership over one's very deepest, most personal intentions. It is the experience of finding oneself repeatedly acting against those very intentions, of finding one's actions themselves robbed of their intended nature in the very moment one commits them.

Paul uses the language of "sin," "flesh," "God," "good," "evil," and "law." However, if we remember that the original meaning of *sin* is a "missing of the mark," what he says can be applied immediately to addiction and codependency as such. We need only read sympathetically, interpreting such terms as *God* in broad generality. Read in that way, his words capture the experience of the disowned self in a way that cannot be improved upon. Accordingly, they provide a fitting end to this chapter.

> For the good that I would do, I do not; but the evil I would not do, that I do. Now if I do that which I would not do, it is no more I that do it, but sin that dwells in me. I find then a law that, when I would do good, evil is present with me. For I delight in the law of God after the inward man; but I see another law in my members, warring against the law of my mind, and bringing me into captivity to the law of sin which is in my members. O wretched man that I am! who shall deliver me from the body of this death?[8]

We return to Paul's question of "delivery" in Part IV, when we consider how to respond to addiction.

· 7 ·

The Meaning of Addiction

Addiction and the Search for Meaning

The pioneering Swiss psychologist Carl G. Jung played a crucial but unintentional role in the formation of Alcoholics Anonymous. In a sense, AA was Jung's great-grandchild. Bill Wilson, co-founder of AA, related the story in a letter to Jung many years after the fact.[1] Wilson wrote the letter in 1961, the last year of Jung's life.

The message that finally released Wilson from the grips of his own alcohol addiction, Wilson wrote Jung, was delivered to him by Edwin ("Ebby") T., an old friend and frequent drinking companion. Ebby, in turn, had received a similar message from a man named Roland H., who had become active in the Oxford Group, an evangelical movement of the time (which eventually changed its name to Moral Rearmament). The man from whom Roland had received that message was Carl Jung.

The story really begins earlier in the 1930s, when Roland H., having sought in vain to control his drinking through various other means, finally became a patient of Jung's. After about a year, he left Jung's care "with a feeling of much confidence" (as Wilson puts it), only to relapse again in a short time. In desperation he returned to Jung, who frankly admitted there was nothing more he could do for him. According to Wilson's account, Jung told Roland that there was no hope of recovery in cases of alcoholism such as his, except for one rather slim chance. That was that Roland "become the subject of a spiritual or religious experience—in short, a genuine conversion." AA owes its existence to the fact that Roland H. shortly experienced just such a conversion.

In his reply to Wilson's letter, Jung gives his own judgment about the meaning of alcoholism. As Jung sees it, in the case of his patient Roland H. (and, by implication, all alcoholics, to one degree or another), "his craving for alcohol was the equivalent, on a low level, of the spiritual thirst of our being for wholeness; expressed in medieval language: the union with God." Jung goes on to share his conviction that "the evil principle prevailing in this world leads the unrecognized spiritual need into perdition if it is not counteracted either by real religious insight or by the protective wall of human community." He then concludes his letter by observing that the Latin term for "alcohol" is *spiritus*. Thus, he writes, "you use the same word for the highest religious experience as well as for the most depraving poison. The helpful formula therefore is: *spiritus contra spiritum* [spirit against spirit]."

There is nothing special about alcoholism that would confine Jung's insight to it. It can be extended to cover addiction in general.

Although his language, tone, and vantage point are all very different, Jung's remarks remind one of William S. Burroughs' observations on how one becomes a drug addict. We have already noted Burroughs' remark that one does not intend to become a drug addict, one just drifts into addiction for lack of any other motivation. It is as if addiction will rush in to fill the vacuum unless strong contrary motivation is present (by way of Jung's religious insight or sense of community, for example).

As we have noted more than once before in reference to Burroughs' comments, drug addiction, alcoholism, and other addictions are certainly not voluntary states. That is, at least in all but the most exceptional cases, no one sets out to become an addict. Nevertheless, as we have also emphasized, one does not become an addict altogether despite oneself, either. Rather, through their own acts addicts ad-dict themselves. They speak themselves over to their addictions in their own repeated choices, however distorted the perceptions underlying those choices may be, as we discussed in the preceding chapter.

Along with speech itself, addiction in the full sense is a distinctively *human* phenomenon. As Stanton Peele and other authors have observed, it is not at all easy to get rats or other animals to display signs of full addiction.[2] In their natural state, or anything even remotely resembling it, there is no evidence of addiction in rats, for example. It is only under the most unnatural laboratory conditions that rats can be induced to dose themselves compulsively with even the most supposedly addictive drugs. Whenever options are available, rats invariably prefer some other, more regularly rat-like behavior. Only the most severely stressed-out rat will shoot up repeatedly.

In contrast to rats, getting human beings to become addicted is remarkably easy. Whereas one really has to force rats to become addicted, about all one has to do to human beings is to give them a chance to become addicts. That, and take away any strong block *against* addiction, as both Jung and Burroughs observe.

The nineteenth-century German philosopher Friedrich Nietzsche remarks that what we humans find intolerable is not pain as such. We can, in fact, tolerate a great deal of pain. What we find intolerable, he notes, is *meaningless* pain.

We need to take Nietzsche one step further. For human beings, we need to add, meaninglessness itself is painful. The *lack* of any clear sense of meaning in life is all it takes to set us off in search of something to fill the gap.

What makes addiction so tempting is precisely that it promises to fill that gap. The problem is that addiction's promises are hollow. Unfortunately, however, once we find that out it is already too late. We are already hooked.

Addicts and Saints

To find meaning in life (or to give it meaning, if one prefers that way of speaking) is not a matter of possessing, but of giving up. It is not a matter of clinging to one's own, but of letting it all go.

In the third century of the Current Era, a young man named Anthony lived in upper Egypt. By the standards of the day, his parents' farm and the income it provided made the family prosperous. Anthony's parents died when he had just entered adulthood. He inherited all of their estate, as well as responsibility for his younger sister.

His parents were committed Christians, and Anthony and his sister were raised to be devout. Shortly after his parents' death,

Anthony proved that he had learned his lesson well—too well, perhaps, at least by worldly standards.

On one of his regular visits to church not long after his parents' death, Anthony had an experience that changed his life forever. The Gospel text for that day was the story of the rich young man who approaches Jesus to ask how he can attain salvation. Jesus tells him that he must follow the well-known commandments and live a devout life. The young man replies that he has done so since his childhood. Jesus then tells him that he lacks only one thing to attain salvation. He must go and sell all he has, and then give the proceeds to the poor and come follow Jesus himself. The young man leaves in obvious dejection.[3]

Listening to this Gospel story, Anthony felt himself spoken to directly. *He* was the rich young man. Like him devout as though by right of birth, Anthony had always lived a godly life. Yet his attachment to his worldly inheritance stood in the middle of his way. That earthly inheritance was blocking him from claiming his heavenly one. Anthony knew what he had to do.

Rushing from the church, he immediately sold his parents' farm and all his other property to give the proceeds to the poor. However, concerned for the welfare of his sister, he kept out just enough to provide for her future.

But then, on his next visit to church, the text for the sermon contained the verse: "Do not be anxious about the morrow."[4] Stricken, Anthony rushed out to give away his last bit of wealth, the part he had held back for his sister. Thereafter, he gave his sister into the care of a group of women in the town who were attempting to live a holy life together as a community and entered into the solitary life for himself. Before long, he quit the precincts of the town altogether and retreated into the desert, first to an old tomb, later to a more distant deserted fort, and finally even deeper into the wasteland. (Soon other spiritual solitaries sought him out, and small communities of monks sprang up near him. In Christian tradition, St. Anthony is remembered as "the Father of monks," a principal source of Christian monasticism.)

Many of us would no doubt find Anthony's behavior incomprehensible, but the addicts among us would understand. (I suspect that William Burroughs and St. Anthony would have gotten on well with one another, despite the former's decidedly non-Christian stance.) Saints and addicts share the same intensity of devotion, the same passion for oblation, for offering oneself up as a living sacrifice. In sum, the passion to give oneself up by speaking oneself over to another is the same.

In both, saints and addicts, there is also the same refusal to settle into complacency. Neither for the saint nor for the addict in us is the response of the young man in the Gospel story acceptable, the cautious response of worldly prudence. It is precisely such caution, such worrying about tomorrow, that St. Anthony emphatically rejects when he gives away even what he had at first held back as insurance against his sister's future needs. Addicts are no more inclined to cling to such insurance than St. Anthony was.

That same episode in the story of St. Anthony also shows how saints do not stop at actions that affect only themselves. They do not hesitate (or, if they do hesitate, they sooner or later overcome such hesitations) to do things that directly affect others, even those for whom they have moral responsibility and to whom they are bound by blood and affection. St. Anthony casts his sister's life into the balance right along with his own.

Addicts are the same. For the sake of their addictions, they do not balk at risking the security of those close to them. They willingly risk their loved ones' security right along with their own. In such regards, the genuine opposite of the addict is not the saint, but the lukewarm, complacent, comfortably "decent" person represented by the rich young man of the Gospel.

It is easy, of course, for such lukewarmness to masquerade behind the facade of "moderation." True moderation, however, has nothing in common with such tepidity. In fact, moderation is really an extreme of its own. Aristotle already knew that. According to him, the general nature of "virtue" is that it is a mean between extremes—the extreme of too much of a given trait, on the one hand, and too little of it, on the other. So, for example, Aristotle says that courage is a mean between the vice of cowardice, where there is so much fear that we are overwhelmed by it, and the vice of foolhardiness, where there is too little fear to keep us out of situations we have no business entering.

Viewed from that perspective, then, virtue is a mean. However, says Aristotle, we can easily shift our perspective a bit. Instead of looking at virtue in terms of the vices it allows us to avoid, we can look at it in terms of the excellence it allows us to achieve. Viewed that way, virtue is seen actually to be the extreme of excellence itself, whereas the vices of excess and deficiency appear as no more than two different ways we can fall short of excellence.[5] In an earlier chapter we noted Aristotle's pertinent observation that there are countless ways to miss the mark, but only one way to hit it dead center.

The hesitancy of the rich young man in the Gospel is not that of the courageous person who pulls back before ill-considered rashness. It is, rather, the anxiety of the fearful person. (Perhaps many of us owe the fact that we are not addicts to the same pusillanimity.)

On the other hand, when St. Anthony gave away the last of his inheritance, leaving even his own sister without any resources of her own, he was not acting in a rash, foolhardy fashion. He was not at all unaware of the risks involved, blinded to them by his initial enthusiasm. If that were the case, his would indeed have been an action of foolhardiness. But Anthony was fully aware of the danger to which he was exposing his sister. That is why he held the money back in the first place. When he did finally give even that remnant up, it was in response to God's voice admonishing him through the scriptures (or, if one prefers, in response to the voice of his own conscience). That voice spoke *against* the voice of Anthony's own fears and reservations, calling him to go forward unreservedly, no longer looking back over his shoulder. For Anthony, not to have heeded that admonishing voice would have been an act of cowardice, not wise caution.

Most of us, when we first hear the story of Anthony, probably see it as extreme. And it is extreme. The question, however, is whether it is the extremity that belongs to vice, or the extremity that belongs to virtue. When we place his behavior in its own proper context, allowing it to have for us the same meaning it had for Anthony, we see that the latter is at issue. We may indeed find Anthony's actions all but incomprehensible. We may even judge him to have been delusional. Nevertheless, we must finally judge him to have been a brave man, rather than a foolhardy one. Certainly the course of action he chose to pursue was not at all the "safe" way to go. However, there is nothing "safe" about virtue, as history repeatedly teaches us. We need only think of such relatively recent examples as Martin Luther King Jr. or Nelson Mandela to understand that. As for the possibility of Anthony's being delusional, the fictional character of Don Quixote shows how little one needs to be free of delusion in order to be an admirable person.

When we view them from the outside and out of the context of meaning that they have for those directly involved, the actions of addicts (and codependents) are often as incomprehensible as St. Anthony's actions are to most of us. Observations such as Jung's about the spiritual meaning of alcoholism suggest, however, that addiction may result from missing the mark of virtue, rather than from aiming at vice—but certainly not from contenting oneself with the comfortable, easy "decency" of the rich young man of the Gospels.

Addiction and the Holy

The Hebrew word for "holiness" is *qōdesh*. What that literally means is "separateness." The holy is that which is set apart, that which is "wholly other," to borrow a well-known phrase from Rudolf Otto, a twentieth-century philosopher of religion. Our word *absolute* says the same thing. *Absolutus* is the past participle of the Latin verb *absolvere*, which consists of *ab*, meaning from, away from, and the root verb *solvere*, which means to loosen or dissolve. Something that is *absolutus* is something that has been loosened and set apart from something else. The holy is that which has been set apart from everything else, set loose from all connections to anything other than itself, separated out as radically other and unique. (It is the absolutely ab-solved, in effect.)

Addiction has about it something of the holy. In *Addiction and Grace*, a book that we have mentioned before, the psychiatrist Gerald May calls addiction "the sacred disease of our time."[6] He is thinking of addiction similarly to the way Jung thought of alcoholism when he said it was an expression of the same longing that, in medieval language, is called the longing for God—a longing for "wholeness," said Jung.

That is another meaning of "holiness." The holy is what is whole.

Our modern English word *holy* comes from Middle English *hool*, which meant healthy, unhurt, entire, whole.

The two meanings of "holiness" (being set apart and being whole) belong together. What is set apart, ab-solved, is what is protected, kept untouched, inviolate. By being set apart, it keeps its "integrity," which literally means "untouchedness."

Addiction sets addicts apart. The alienation that is a fundamental experiential characteristic of addiction sets them apart from others and from themselves. That characteristic points directly to the dis-own-ment that is the very essence of addiction, and which radically separates addicts not just from their families, communities, and everyday selves, but also from everything "proper" to them—everything that could be called their "own."

Illness of any sort sets a person apart. To be ill means to be absolved from the daily round of healthy, active life. One of the traditional Christian sacraments is anointing the sick. Such anointing is not some attempt magically to restore health. It is, rather, a way of acknowledging the set-apart-ness, the holiness, that attaches to the sick as such. By anointing with oil in a ritual setting, the community as a whole, through the celebrant, marks the sick with an "effective sign" of their sacredness, the signifying of which actually sanctifies (sacramentalizes) those on whom it is bestowed.

As illness, addiction already sets addicts apart, making them different, special. But addicts' disdain of everyday complacency and comfortable conformity to social norms also marks them as different even from the sick in general. The apparent extremism of addiction, when viewed from the standards of the everyday, marks addicts as distinctively as the comparable extremism of the saints marks them.

The very uncanniness of addiction, the frightening foreignness of it to our everyday understanding, testifies to the connection of addiction to the holy. It is not that addiction itself is holy, at least not in the same way that God is holy in Judeo-Christian-Islamic thought. Rather, the holiness that belongs to God in that tradition is the mark the *missing* of which shoots one over *into* addiction. But just as the sinner is closer to heaven than the self-righteous, conventionally upright person, so is the addict closer to holiness than the person who avoids addiction only at the price of never reaching for the absolute. Only repentance separates the sinner from salvation, whereas the self-righteous person refuses even to acknowledge that there is any need for repentance. Similarly, in order finally to hit the holy mark, the addict who, in the words of the old Peggy Lee song, would rather keep drinking, or drugging, or otherwise practicing addiction, "if that's all there is," just needs to learn where to look truly to find the "more" he or she has always been seeking.

The book *Alcoholics Anonymous* says that AA members are not saints. It says that they can claim only "progress, not perfection."[7] That may well be, but still the alcoholic or other addict stands in the shadow of the saint. In contrast, those who have never been addicted only because they lack enough passion for it are not even in sainthood's vicinity.

The "Grateful Alcoholic"

Some AA members use that self-identification when they introduce themselves before speaking at an AA meeting. "Hi!" they will say, "I'm Joe" (or Jean, or Fran, or whoever), "and I'm a grateful alcoholic."

But what is there to be grateful for in being an alcoholic?

Even if, as addicts, alcoholics do stand in close, albeit perverse, proximity to saints, there is no denying the misery, pain, and suffering that go with alcoholism. Not just for codependents, but above all for alcoholics themselves, alcoholism is anything but a desirable condition. No one in his or her right mind would wish alcoholism on anyone.

Most AA newcomers are not at all grateful for being alcoholics. For that matter, most are not grateful for much of anything when they walk into their first AA meeting. The last place in the world they want to be is where they are—in a room full of sober ex-drunks who seem happy to be that way. And for a long time many newcomers continue to ask "Why me?" They bewail their fate. Pitying themselves fiercely, they wonder aloud why *they* have to be alcoholics when they see others "drinking with impunity," as it is put in *Alcoholics Anonymous*.[8]

Eventually, however, if such newcomers "keep coming back," as they are told to do at the end of almost any AA meeting anywhere, they will find their attitude changing. They will begin to be happy in their own sobriety. They will find themselves not just *being* sober, but actually *enjoying* it. They will see their lives improve in many unexpected ways, and they will begin to appreciate the tremendous freedom that comes from no longer having to pick up the next drink.

When they reach that point, newcomers might even come to speak of how "grateful" they are for a variety of things: for finding their way to AA, for learning how to live without alcohol, for having discovered or rediscovered a relationship to a "higher power," or whatever. At this stage they may even be willing to characterize themselves as grateful in general. However, most are still unwilling to express any gratitude for their alcoholism as such. They may say such things as that they are grateful for their *recovery* from alcoholism, and for all the good things that accompany recovery. But they still insist that they are not grateful for their alcoholism as such. If they had had their way, they will say, they would never have suffered from alcoholism in the first place, so they would never have needed to "recover" from it, either.

AA members may never grow beyond that stage. They may live generally happy, productive, and, above all, sober lives from that point forward, without their attitude towards their alcoholism undergoing any further change. Some, however, do grow beyond that stage into a stage of being grateful for their alcoholism itself.

There is an old joke about how to teach a mule something. First you have to get an axe handle and whack him over the head with it as hard as you can, the joke goes. That way you'll get his attention. It may be that some of us are just so mulish by nature or circumstance that the only way whatever powers are responsible for our ultimate welfare can get our attention is by whacking us over the head with a large enough axe handle. For some of us, alcoholism or some other equally destructive addiction may be the only axe handle large enough for the purpose.

Being hit in the head with an axe handle hurts, to be sure. There's no denying that. But if that's what it takes to get our attention so we can be pointed in the right direction to find what we've always been looking for (even if we never even knew we were looking for it), then we might very well be grateful for it anyway.

Addiction as the Cure for Idolatry

Addiction gets the addict's attention. The deeper the addiction, the more exclusively it captures the addict's attention. In the deepest forms of addiction, the addict barely pays attention to anything else.

Then, when the addiction has really captured the addict's attention, the addict is finally ready to learn something. Addiction then turns out to be even more than the axe handle that was big enough to get the addict's attention. Addiction also turns out to be the teacher of the lesson the learning of which justifies all the effort to attract that attention.

The lesson addiction has to teach is if "all there is" were the sorts of things Peggy Lee sings about in her song, then there really would be no reason not to keep right on drinking and drugging; but that's *not* "all there is." What there really is only starts to become clear when one takes all that—takes all those things the song is about—and throws them away.

An addict is a person who always wants *more.* Not "more of the same," more of the daily round of gains and losses, of goods and services that suffice for most of us most of the time, but "more" in the sense of something altogether different, something no longer measurable by such everyday standards—something "more than all that."

It is because addiction involves this longing for the incommensurably "more" that it strikes the well-to-do no less than the destitute. Addiction is an equal opportunity disowner. For the adolescent on the streets in the ghetto, addiction promises an escape from the dead-end hopelessness of the cycle of poverty. It offers something more. But it is no less the case that addiction promises escape from the restrictive complacency of middle-class suburbia, or from the hollowness of conventional success, so that it can also appeal to the person who apparently "has it all." Addiction provides a ghoulish answer to the question of what to give such a person. Once again, it offers something more.

Addiction is the "algebra of need," as Burroughs says in his well-known novel *Naked Lunch.*[9] Addictive need is a need that can never be satisfied by any amount of money, approval, power, wealth, health, speed, or risk. That is because it is a need, as Jung saw, that nothing less than God (to use "medieval language," as Jung calls it) can satisfy. As Gregory Bateson in effect also perceived, addiction is the living out of such an incommensurable need. For that very reason, as Bateson saw further, it is the process that progressively weans addicts away from any substitutes for the absolute. Once addicts live the addictive process through to its natural end—an end, however, that may all too often prove to lie "the other side of death," as Bateson remarks—they are at last freed from all illusion that there can be any substitutes for God (or *nirvana*, the Self, the Void, or whatever other name one uses for the same ab-solute no-thing that alone can satisfy the addict's need).

Viewed from that perspective, addiction is the cure for idolatry.

The rich young man of the Gospels, the one whose attachment to his wealth keeps him from salvation, is a fitting image of an idolater whose idolatry has truly become hopeless. The problem with his idolatry, what makes it so hopeless, so closed to the very possibility of recovery, is precisely that it is so comfortable to him. He is completely at home with his wealth. He enjoys the many fine things it allows him to have, including the good conscience that comes with the regular almsgiving and the other accompaniments of righteous living that his wealth makes possible for him—and not only possible, but even easy. It is his very wealth that allows him to be "good." Thanks to his wealth, that very goodness really costs *him* nothing.

In contrast, were the same young man to come into a genuinely *addictive* relationship to his wealth, a ray of hope might paradoxically shine into his hopelessness. His wealth might then cease to be a mere instrument for his pleasure and for preserving his good image of himself. He might cease to value it for what it could bring him. He might come to relate to it as an end in itself. All his thoughts might come constantly to return to his wealth, and to turn around it. He might sell all his own comfort, and the comfort of those dear to him, for its sake. His wealth might become, for him, the absolute. It might become the God he passionately worshiped, demanding everything of him—instead of what his wealth actually is for the rich young man in the Gospel story: the comfortable means for him to maintain his complacency.

Søren Kierkegaard draws a portrait of the comfortable, upright, righteous, churchgoing citizen of nineteenth-century Danish Christendom, who has every particle of proper theological doctrine down pat, but whose professed Christianity costs him nothing. Kierkegaard contrasts such passionless self-righteousness with the condition of a superstitious, pagan idol worshiper, who has every bit of theological doctrine wrong, but who puts his whole heart into passionate devotion to his idol. The deluded idol worshiper, says Kierkegaard, is far closer to God than the correct-thinking citizen of Christendom. The very passion and wholeheartedness of the former's worship brings him into proximity to God, says Kierkegaard. In contrast, combined with his cold sense of righteousness, the very correctness of view and behavior of the member of nineteenth-century Christendom drives him away from God.

Kierkegaard's idol worshiper is an addict. If he ever "hits bottom" in the addictive process, then he will find himself right where he has always wanted to be: in the bosom of God himself. Paradoxically, when lived out to its end in such a fashion, the process of addiction proves itself to be a process of iconoclasm, the destruction of idols. Because it pushes addicts always to seek an incommensurable "something more," addiction never lets addicts settle down in anything less than the absolute, the way the rich young man of the Gospels and Kierkegaard's member of Danish Christendom settle down in their comfortable righteousness.

The Meaning of Addiction

As we saw in the preceding chapter, addiction in essence is an enslaving disownment. It is an existential condition that, primarily through one's own, never consciously thought-out actions, divests one of ownership over one's own life. Addicts are no longer their "own persons." They have come to belong to their addictions.

However, what we have been discussing in this chapter is that the impetus behind addiction is to be found in a radical dissatisfaction with everyday "reality," a dissatisfaction with anything relative. Addiction reveals a longing for the absolute.

If it were not for that longing, addiction would lose all its appeal. It would cease to have the experientially tempting, tranquilizing, and disburdening qualities that draw potential addicts into addiction in the first place. That, perhaps, is the major reason that rats and other animals prove impervious to addiction in their natural conditions, displaying addictive (or at least addiction-like) behaviors only under the most artificially confining laboratory conditions. It may be because they lack what Camus called the "wild longing in the human heart" that they are not at risk of becoming addicts.

By appearing to offer "something more"—"more" in a nonaddictive way incommensurable with the reality of everyday—addiction promises to still that longing. It creates the illusion of having found one's way home, having at last found the "one thing lacking" to make one whole. It is the illusion of having entered the state of pure communion one has always been seeking, the illusion of having found God himself—or the way to do without God altogether.

To address that perpetual human longing for "something more" is the offer through which addiction tempts us. To have stilled this longing feeling is the illusion with which addiction tranquilizes us. To bear it is the burden of which addiction disburdens us. Together, the tempting, tranquilizing, and disburdening qualities of addiction are the hook by which addiction hooks us.

As soon as it has hooked us, the emptiness of addiction's offer begins to become apparent. So does the illusoriness of the feeling it gives us; and it begins to lay upon us a new and far heavier burden. By then, however, it is too late. After all, by then we *are* hooked; addiction now proves to have alienated us from ourselves and others, and above all from the object of that very longing without which addiction could never have hooked us at the start. When we struggle to "come to ourselves" again, like the prodigal son in another Gospel story, addiction only entangles us all the more. All the while it dissembles its operations, perpetuating itself through our very efforts to free ourselves from it.

Thus, as Jung saw, addiction proves to be a distortion or perversion of the longing for what is radically "more." As we noted at the beginning of this chapter, Jung attributes the perverting of this longing to "the evil principle prevailing in this world" working on "the unrecognized spiritual need" in question. We return to the role that the failure to *recognize* the spiritual need at issue plays in addiction in the final part of this book, when we consider what responses are appropriate to addiction, but here we only wish to borrow Jung's idea of an inexplicable "evil principle" at work in turning spiritual longing into addiction.

We need only to borrow that idea, not keep it. Furthermore, we borrow it only to set the stage for introducing another idea, one that Jung himself does not mention. That idea, common to all nondualistic religious traditions, including Christianity, is that the opposing *positive* power is so great and so uncanny as always to be able to turn even the worst machinations of Jung's negative "evil principle" against its own intentions, and to bring good rather than evil out of them. By this idea, the devil has always lost the game in advance, even before it begins. His opponent is somehow, in utterly unforseeable ways, always able to turn the devil's very most cunningly evil moves into even greater good.

So, in the case of addiction, the very process of enslavement, if only followed out to its natural end, brings the addict into the very opposite condition, that of liberation. At the heart of disownment, one is unexpectedly brought into one's own. By stripping addicts of everything, even and above all themselves, addiction eventually leaves them with nowhere else to turn except toward "God as one understands God," to paraphrase a crucial expressions from AA's Twelve Steps. By radically dis-owning addicts of themselves, addiction ends up stripping them of everything that stands in the way of their becoming what in God's eye they already are, and have always been, to borrow another phrase, this one from the poet Gerard Manley Hopkins. The addict who has finally hit bottom has "nothing left to lose," which, to end this spate of borrowings by taking a line this time from Janis Joplin, is just another way of saying that such an addict is finally free. At that point addicts are given the rare opportunity to live their own lives, and live them abundantly, no longer letting any idols live them out for them.

Thus, when the addict finally "hits bottom," addiction turns out to be a paradoxically liberating process of enslavement in which one comes to oneself through losing oneself utterly. In that sense, the meaning of addiction is freedom.

However, freedom—genuine freedom—can never be forced on anyone. It always comes in the form of a choice.

Addiction eventually confronts addicts with a clear and fundamental choice. It is *fundamental* because it consists of the choice of either choosing to *have* a choice in the first place, or of refusing to choose at all. Thus, in another sense than what we have just been considering, the "meaning" of addiction depends upon the specifics of the given case. What addiction in any given actual case turns out to mean depends on what one does, when one has finally "hit bottom." At that point one is at last confronted with the fact that one truly does have a choice. But one can either accept that fact by actually *choosing*, and thereby reclaiming choice itself as one's own, or turn one's back on choosing by remaining in the addiction (and all the self-pity that so easily goes with it).

The meaning of addiction is freedom precisely because addiction drives the addict to such an existential turning point. From that point on, however, the meaning of addiction is up to the addict.

·8·

The Root of Addiction

Roots and Causes

The causes of something are the external conditions that bring it about. Causes are events that produce or bring about other events. For example, a lightning strike in a dry forest can cause a fire, pushing a properly functioning doorbell button causes the doorbell to ring, and stress can cause headaches. In each case, the cause is one event, what it causes—the "effect"—is another event.

Sometimes, we apply the notion of cause to individual events, and sometimes we apply it to classes of events. So, for example, in a given case of death the cause of death may be a heart attack, in another case a stroke, and in a third case it may be kidney failure. Yet we also say simply that heart attacks cause death, and so do strokes and kidney failures.

When we are discussing classes of events, as in the last examples, we are not dealing with invariant connections. Thus, heart attacks do not always cause death, nor do strokes, nor kidney failures. Far from being invariant, the connections between those three illnesses and death are subject to very wide variation.

When we say that such things as heart attacks cause death, we don't even mean that they "generally" cause it. That is, we don't necessarily mean that even *most* heart attacks cause death. Even if most heart attacks do not result in death for those who suffer them, we still feel quite comfortable claiming that heart attacks cause death.

Accordingly, simply from knowing that heart attacks "cause" death, we cannot arrive at any sound conclusion concerning any individual's actual death or the results of any actual heart attack. Knowing that heart attacks cause death doesn't tell us what caused any given death, nor does it tell us that any given heart attack will cause death.

In fact, about all that we really mean when we say that heart attacks cause death is that there is a direct connection between the two such that, given certain *other* conditions (which may actually occur only relatively infrequently), a heart attack will produce or bring about death. Those other conditions include such things as the general health (aside from the heart trouble) of the person having the attack, the availability of medical assistance, the severity of the attack, and so forth. When we say that heart attacks cause death, all we really mean is that, if we keep all those other conditions constant, the incidence of death in any given population will vary directly with the incidence of heart attacks in that same population. Thus, if the number of heart attacks increases, while all the other factors remain unchanged, then the number of deaths will also increase; and if the former decreases, then so will the latter. (Even then, there would be no one-to-one correspondence. Not every new heart attack would necessarily bring about a new death, for example.)

When we are dealing with the causal analysis of general social phenomena, we are almost always in that position. So, for instance, if we want to know what causes theft, we will soon see that one cause of theft is poverty. That is, if other factors are held the same, the incidence of theft in a society in general will rise with the incidence of poverty. From that alone, however, we can never justify the conclusion that a given act of theft is the result of poverty. Nor can we conclude that anyone who lives in poverty must be a thief.

So much for our quick review of the notion of causes. We now turn to the notion of *roots*. In contrast to its causes, the roots of a given phenomenon are not external factors that are capable of producing it. Instead, the roots of a phenomenon belong to that phenomenon itself. To use the definitive example, the roots of a plant are not something apart from the plant, something external that produces the plant as an effect. Rather, the roots of a plant are themselves part of the plant. They are the part of the plant that anchors it in the soil. It is from the same soil, furthermore, that the roots also draw the nutrients the plant needs to live. As the plant grows, so do the roots. Conversely, if the roots wither, the plant dies.

In the same way, the roots of a phenomenon are the underlying anchoring and sustaining depths of the phenomenon itself. As roots, they belong to the phenomenon as inseparable, indispensable parts. The causes of a phenomenon may cease to exist no sooner than they have produced the phenomenon as their effect, but the roots of a phenomenon must continue to exist if the phenomenon itself is to do so.

For most if not all phenomena, there is more than one conceivable cause. That is, for most phenomena, there are any number of conditions that will produce that phenomenon—bring it forth in the first place. Regardless of how it is caused, however, the phenomenon itself remains the same, and so do its roots.

The Causes of Addiction

In general, in thinking about the causes of addiction we do not need to add much to a formulation by the neuroscientist Avram Goldstein,[1] whom we have cited before. Goldstein's formulation explicitly addresses drug addiction, but what he says can easily be extended to cover addiction of any kind. "There is obviously no single, simple cause of addiction," writes Goldstein. Rather, he continues, "The contributions of three main factors will determine, at a particular time and place, the incidence and prevalence of addiction to a given drug."

The first of those three factors is the most obvious, and the one on which most American governmental efforts to stem drug addiction focus: "Availability of the drug." All other things being equal, the more readily available a drug is to a given population, the higher will be the incidence of addiction to that drug within the same population. The prevalence of alcoholism, nicotine addiction, and caffeine addiction in contemporary Western societies demonstrates the importance of this factor.

Second, the incidence of drug addiction will be a function of "individual predisposition to use the drug repeatedly and to become addicted." We combine discussion of this second factor with that of Goldstein's third, which is: "External faciliatory and inhibitory factors such as societal, family, religious, and cultural traditions and attitudes, legal restraints, stressful or tranquil conditions of life, and alternative sources of satisfaction."

Research can add only limited new insights into the operation of the first factor, the availability of the drugs or their equivalents to which addiction occurs in the given setting. However, research can and already has added a great deal to flesh out each of the other two factors.

Under the second general factor—individual predisposition toward addiction to the given drug or its equivalent—much research has been done, and is continuing to be done, into *genetic* factors in addiction. Thus, for example, it has long been known that the children of alcoholics run four to five times greater risk of becoming alcoholics themselves than do the children of nonalcoholics. The evidence is that that is so even for children of alcoholics who were put out for adoption and raised in nonalcoholic families. Such evidence makes a strong suggestion that there are genetic factors at work. Recently, scientists have even made some headway in identifying specific genes that may predispose one toward alcoholism. As general evidence of the role of genetic determinants in human health and behavior continues to mount, it is not at all surprising that such evidence is also surfacing in the case of alcoholism and other addictions.

Nevertheless, it is very important not to become confused by all the recent talk of an "alcoholism gene" and the like. What is at issue in such cases is a genetic *predisposition*. There is not at all any *necessity* involved, such that anyone born with the so-called alcoholism gene, for instance, is doomed sooner or later to become addicted to alcohol, provided only that alcohol be available. As in the case of poverty causing theft, nothing of the sort is involved. At the most, what is involved is no more than an increased incidence of alcoholism among those who are born with the gene at issue. In general, the bottom line is that most children of alcoholics do *not* become alcoholics themselves; and there is no evidence at all to support the contention that there is some gene that guarantees that those who have it will become alcoholics, given the opportunity, despite themselves.

To reinforce this point, let us consider an apparently extreme case. One author has recently suggested that alcoholism is not only "hereditary," but even "inherited"—that is, that alcoholism as such, and not just the predisposition toward it, is genetically transmitted.[2] However, that claim depends upon the author in question drawing a sharp distinction between "alcoholism" and "alcohol addiction," in accordance with which alcohol*ism* is equivalent to the predisposition toward alcohol *addiction*. Thus, a merely terminological disagreement disguises an underlying substantive agreement with the position that actual *addiction* to alcohol is *not* hereditary. (It is important to keep in mind the terminological convention adopted throughout this book—a common one in which *alcoholism* and *alcohol addiction* are used interchangeably.)

In sum, at most what we are dealing with in such genetic factors still remains an instance of what Goldstein has already correctly labeled "individual predisposition to use the drug repeatedly and to become addicted." Put differently, what we have in such cases are individual *risk factors* for addiction. The situation is really the same as when we talk about overweight, smoking, family history of heart problems, stress, and the like being risk factors for heart disease.

In addition to genetic predisposition, this category of risk factors that vary at the individual level includes psychological personality factors.[3] So, for example, research has shown that alcoholic drinkers as a group tend to be more "field dependent" and to have a more "external locus of control" than do nonalcoholic drinkers. To be field dependent means to take one's cues for how to behave from outside oneself, such as from the reactions of others, rather than from one's own desires, emotions, and autonomous motivations. To have an external locus of control means to perceive oneself as largely at the mercy of powers beyond one's own control, rather than largely able to control one's own destiny (an "internal locus of control").

Accordingly, field dependency and the tendency to have an external locus of control can both be identified as "causes" of addiction. That is, each is a "risk factor" for addiction.

Goldstein's second general factor determining "the incidence and prevalence of addiction" is, then, the category of all such risk factors (whether genetic, psychological, matters of mere taste and preference, or whatever) that vary at the level of individual persons. In turn, Goldstein's third category of causes for addiction—"external faciliatory and inhibitory factors"—presents us with another set of risk factors. In distinction to those we have just been considering, however, this new category is that of *social* risk factors,[4] as Goldstein's examples make clear: "societal, family, religious and cultural traditions and attitudes, legal restraints, stressful or tranquil conditions of life, and alternative sources of satisfaction."

Each of Goldstein's examples identifies a different subclass of social causes or risk factors of addiction. Thus, the first subclass is that of social traditions, customs, and attitudes, "mores," in the broad sense. The second subclass is that of formal legal sanctions directed against addiction. The third is that of economic factors, again in the broad sense of that term. Following Jung's insight that addictive perversion of spiritual longing will occur unless blocked by genuine spiritual experience or strong communal ties, we might call the final subclass suggested by Goldstein's list that of spiritual-communal factors.

Although he does not expressly list it in the passage at issue along with his other three general factors, Goldstein's own research makes it clear that a fourth important factor is also at play in determining the incidence of addiction at a particular time for a particular population. That is the factor of the objective properties of the substances or activities to which addiction occurs.

In an earlier chapter, we pointedly rejected the idea that addiction can be accounted for simply by the properties of the objects of addiction. As we said there, such an idea is really just a modern way of demonizing addiction. It is clearly incompatible with an understanding of the *existential* nature of addiction.

That is not to say, however, that the properties of the objects to which addiction occurs are altogether irrelevant for giving a causal account of addiction. Rather, given the existential nature of addiction and its meaning, only substances and activities having certain general properties will prove suitable as potential objects of addiction.

It is no accident, for example, that the drugs to which addiction most frequently occurs are either stimulants or depressants (or each in turn biphasically, as with alcohol). In contrast, there is a far lower incidence of addiction to hallucinogenic drugs such as LSD (which is not to deny that taking such drugs may be potentially seriously harmful in other ways).

Those observations raise two questions. The first is how addiction can occur so easily to both depressants and stimulants, since the physiological effects of those two different types of drug are opposite to one another. The second question is why addiction does not occur anywhere near as readily with drugs that are neither depressants nor stimulants, but that are nevertheless "psychoactive" (that is, have a very definite mood-altering effect).

Stanton Peele offers good answers to both questions that are quite compatible with an existential understanding of addiction. "Addictive experiences," Peele notes in one of his works, "are not random; people become addicted to experiences that have clear cut and specifiable elements." He then goes on to observe the importance of mood alteration: "First and foremost, addictive experiences are potent modifiers of mood and sensation, in part because of their direct pharmacological action or physical impact and in part because of their learned or symbolic significance."[5]

As we already remarked in an earlier chapter, mood alteration certainly plays a role in the genesis of addiction, even though addiction cannot be accounted for simply as the result of mood-altering properties of addictive objects. If a drug or an activity did not have some noticeable mood-altering effect—if it did not "do" something to us—then we would hardly be tempted to addict ourselves to that drug or that activity.

To that extent, however, there seems to be no difference between depressants and stimulants, on one hand, and hallucinogenic drugs, on the other. They all produce mood alterations. Indeed, in the doses commonly taken, hallucinogens such as LSD are often more powerfully mood altering than are common dosages of most depressants or stimulants.

What distinguishes hallucinogens from depressants and stimulants, however, is that the mood-altering effects of hallucinogens are far less predictable than those of depressants and stimulants (at least as those effects are experienced by typical users). Depressants are depressingly regular in their experienced action. Stimulants are no less stimulating in their regularity.

For both depressants and stimulants, "(but not hallucinogens)," as Peele notes in another work, "an artificial sameness is the key-

note of the addictive experience."[6] Although they work in physiologically opposite ways, both depressants and stimulants provide
such sameness. Both provide a way of regulating the organism's
level of excitation, keeping it constant. It is precisely such sameness,
such routine repeatability, that the addict seeks in the object of
addiction. Since hallucinogens do not have that property of sameness, they have little or no addictive appeal.

At the same time, there is another difference (one Peele does not
stress). Stimulants and depressants both work directly on moods.
In contrast, hallucinogens, as their very name implies, work directly
on perception and only indirectly on moods. It is only insofar as the
drug user responds emotionally to the hallucinations engendered by
taking the drug that hallucinogens as such have a mood-altering
effect. As noted previously, what addicts want is what stimulants
and depressants provide (once again, at least as addicts experience
it): the direct manipulation of their own moods.

Thus, among the many causes of addiction—among the many
risk factors for it—is this capacity of commonly addictive substances and processes to provide mood alteration combined with
this "artificial sameness" of experience. All other things being
equal, the incidence of addiction will vary with the degree to which
this property is present in whatever substances and processes are
(Goldstein's first factor again) available.

Objects of addiction (the fourth factor, the one just considered),
addicts themselves (Goldstein's second factor), the availability of
the former to the latter (his first factor), and the social setting in
which they are available (his third)—the various causes or risk
factors for addiction must all fit into one of those four categories.
Beyond those four categories, there is no place left in which such
causes might be found. Users, what they use, whether it is there to
be used in the first place, and the mores that mediate its usage
exhaust the possibilities.

It is important to remember that none of these four factors of
cause operates in isolation from the others in the production of
addiction. Indeed, the interconnection between them is so close that
it is often impossible to identify the operation of one factor in clear
separation from the operation of one or more of the others.

For example, the contribution of the last factor we have considered, pertaining to the actual properties of objects of addiction,

cannot, in concrete cases of addiction, be separated from contributions that belong to the second factor, individual predisposition toward addiction. One such individual matter is the set of *expectancies* that given persons bring to their experience with given substances or processes. Pertaining to such expectancies, studies have suggested that the drinking behavior of groups of alcoholics may be more affected by the fact that they *think* they are drinking alcohol than by the fact that they actually *are*.[7] We have also discussed what we called the "existential equation of addiction," in accordance with which addicts learn to *equate* practicing their addictions with "feeling all right," irrespective of what their objective physiological reactions may actually be.

Accordingly, maintaining the constant level of excitation that Peele talks about is never simply a matter of the objective properties of a given drug or the like. Rather, it is a matter of the complex interplay of those properties with the subjective experience *of* them by the individual addict.

In turn, that subjective experience is mediated by a number of social factors. The expectancies one has about taking a given drug are affected not only by one's own previous experiences with it, but also (and often even more so) by what one's society, family, or peer group has taught one to expect.

The availability of the given object of addiction (Goldstein's first factor) in a given society depends in large part on such things as the legal sanctions imposed upon possession of it, how socially acceptable it is, and so forth (his third factor). Furthermore, just how "available" a drug or other object of addiction really needs to be for a given addict to continue the addiction depends on such individual matters as how strongly the addict wants it (the second factor). One addict will put up with much more trouble to maintain the supply than will another. Once again, what occurs in any concrete case is the result of the complex interplay between the various factors.[8]

The Root of Addiction

In following Peele's account of why addiction occurs with both depressants and stimulants but not with hallucinogens, we have already touched on something that pertains to the root of addiction.

According to Peele, what makes a drug inviting for addiction is that it offers addicts a way to control their own level of experienced excitation, regardless of the circumstances in which they find themselves. Through the use of depressant or stimulant drugs, addicts are able to keep that level constant, even when the world is coming down around their ears. They are thus able to experience a sense of control over their own reaction to events that affect them negatively, as painful or undesirable. By the same token, through using the very same drugs addicts are also able to experience the same sense of control over their own reactions to events that affect them positively, as pleasant or desirable.

As the reminder about the role of expectancies in addiction lets us see, what really counts for addicts is not that their level of excitation actually *be* constant, as judged by objective standards, but that they subjectively *experience* it as constant. More to the point, addicts experience *themselves* as *able to keep it constant* by practicing their addictions.

The key element is the experience of *a sense of control*. In a recent book on AA's Twelve Steps, psychologist J. Keith Miller, himself a recovering alcoholic, refers to his addiction as "my control disease."[9] Indeed, any addiction, whether to alcohol, other substances, or processes, is such a disease. To whatever else they may be addicted, all addicts are addicted to "control." They are addicted, that is, to *the experience of the sense of being "in control" or "under control,"* that very experience the taking of stimulants and depressants, for example, but not hallucinogens, provides them.

Precisely *where* a given addict will turn to find that experience depends upon the interplay of the four categories of causal factors we have just finished discussing. Depending on the properties of the various potential objects of addiction available, individual predisposition, and social mediation, one person will turn to alcohol, another to heroin. Yet a third will even turn to jogging. In whatever direction each turns, what the turn to addiction in general provides every addict is a way of maintaining the same sense of being in control.

At bottom, *that* is why both stimulants and depressants are likely candidates for objects of addiction. What finally counts is not using either class of drugs to keep one's level of excitation constant for its own sake. What counts is using them constantly to keep one's sense of being in control. It is only insofar as the sense of being in control is incompatible with a level of excitation experienced as fluctuating *beyond* one's control that keeping one's excitation level constant plays a role in addiction.

Furthermore, to become addicted to something is precisely to come to a point where one feels "out of control" whenever one is not allowed to practice the addiction, but where one feels "in control" whenever one does practice it. Thus, it is the desire to experience this sense of being in control that explains the "existential equation of addiction" we formulated earlier: For addicts, to feel "all right" *is* to practice the addiction, and not to practice it is *not* to feel "all right," because it is only when practicing the addiction, but then always, that addicts feel *in control*.

The sense of being in control that is at issue in every addiction is that of being in control of *oneself*. It is not necessary that practicing one's addiction give one any grand illusions that one is in control of others or of events in general. Every addiction involves an addiction to control, but not every addict is a "control junkie." That is, not all addicts are people who feel comfortable only when they experience themselves as in control of everything going on around them. Not every addict tries to control conversations, "figure angles," or do the other sorts of thing we associate with the "controller" or "control freak." The latter are indeed addicts, whose addiction is, however, to the manipulation of situations and other people. Control addicts in that sense are people who feel in control of *themselves* only when they are controlling others, just as alcoholics feel in control of themselves only when they are drinking, heroin addicts only when they are shooting up, or sex addicts only when they are acting out.

This need to feel in control of oneself is also what will allow us to account for the role in addiction of what might best be called "attributions." It will allow us to see that there is a root addiction to "attribution" that is itself at the root of all addiction.

"Attribution" and Addiction

In what has become the classic experiment concerning attributions, groups of college student volunteers were told they were needed for a study of the effects of a harmless drug. Then they were given injections of epinephrine, more commonly known as adrenaline, the drug that anger and related emotions release into the bloodstream. The drug increases the pulse, constricts the blood vessels, and, in general, sets the organism on the lookout for danger, putting it in a "fight or flight" mode of response.

In the experiment, one group of students was told what was in the injection and informed of the physiological reactions it was to expect. When they experienced those symptoms on cue, those students dismissed them as no more than the effects of the drug.

However, another group of students was given the same injection, but was not provided with information about its contents or what effects, if any, to expect from it. One of the purported volunteers was actually a plant, an actor who was paid to pretend to feel anger at the appropriate time, just when the epinephrine began to take effect. In that group, the real volunteers showed a marked tendency to interpret what they were feeling as caused by anger of their own, rather than by the recent injection of the drug. The volunteers themselves thought they also were angry; they "attributed" the symptoms they were experiencing to that cause.[10]

The researchers drew some far-reaching conclusions from the results of their experiment, conclusions that continue to be widely disputed and which need not concern us. All that we need to take from the experiment is its clear illustration of the notion of *attribution*.

The experiment actually demonstrates at least two clear sequences of attributions, one following the other. Even before the students in the second group attributed their sensations to anger of their own, they had already made another attribution. They had attributed the facial expression, gestures, and other behavior of the planted actor to anger on *his* part. The truth of the matter was that the actor was not experiencing any anger, but was only acting out his assigned role. The other members of the group (wrongly) attributed his behavior to anger they took him to be feeling, just as they then took that as an unconscious cue to (wrongly) attribute the sensations they were feeling at the time to anger of their own.

If we wanted, we could even say that five distinct moments of attribution are at play in the experiment, not just two. That is, we could divide it as follows: (1) An attribution occurs when the students first observe the actor's behavior: They attribute that behavior to an emotion, anger (rather than, say, to the sorts of uncontrollable outbursts that belong to the condition called Tourette syndrome). That is, the attribution made here is that the behavior is "anger behavior." (2) Another attribution then occurs when the students judge that the planted actor actually *is* angry (rather than just pretending to be angry, perhaps, which would still be compatible with interpreting his behavior as "anger behavior" in accordance with the first attribution). (3) On the basis of their double attribution concerning the actor, the volunteers next attribute their own sensations to anger (parallel to the first attribution, where they attribute not their own sensations to anger, but the observed behavior of another person to it). (4) They then attribute their own actual anger to themselves (rather than, for example, treating their symptoms as some sort of interesting empathetic reaction triggered in them by observing the anger behavior of the actor, but not making them genuinely angry themselves). (5) Finally, they search around in their experience of the present situation, or look back in memory, until they can find something they can make serve as the "cause" of their supposed anger. They interpret their anger as anger "at" or "because of" that thing. (It, whatever it turns out to be, "made" them angry.)

We are all incessantly making attributions of one sort or another. That is, we are all constantly *interpreting* our experience, and not just neutrally recording it. We interpret the behavior of others, both verbal and nonverbal, attributing motives or the lack of motives to them. "She is saying that *because* she is angry." "He did that *because* he was afraid." "They would only do a thing like that *because* they don't know what they're doing." We also interpret our own actions, as well as our own physical sensations, attributing them to motives or the lack of motives in ourselves. "I said that only *because* I was excited." "My stomach is growling *because* I'm hungry." No less do we interpret the behavior of animals, as well as occurrences in nature, attributing everything to some underlying other thing. There is always some "because."

The very fabric of our daily lives is woven of attributions. Furthermore, the whole of modern science is nothing but a cloth made up of countless attributions methodically arrived at and systematically interconnected, a cloth continually being mended, broadened, and bordered, being stitched, unstitched, then stitched up anew.

Interpersonal relations are also knitted together by strings of attributions, as are the pieces in our images of ourselves. In the privacy of our own minds, when we are completely still and wholly unoccupied by outside activities, alone with our deepest selves, our very thoughts are strung together by no different thread.

"Wherever you go, there you are," runs an amusing line sometimes popular in Alcoholics Anonymous and other addiction recovery groups. And wherever you are, we might well add, there you go—there you go, that is, making attributions. We cannot stop making them. We are addicted to them. When we are deprived of the opportunity to make attributions, we feel like we are coming apart. We feel just like the junky who needs a fix but can't find a connection.

One good way of defining what we experience as genuinely "uncanny" is that anything we cannot *attribute* to something is uncanny. We dread it. Attributions let us feel that we understand what is going on in and around us; and when we understand what is going on in and around us, we feel in control of ourselves. We may not like what is going on. We may not like it at all. But if we feel we understand it, at least it no longer has the power to fill us with dread.

Of course, not every attribution is mistaken, like that of the students who attributed their injection-induced symptoms to anger. Many attributions are correct, and science and scholarship provide us with methods for maximizing the chances our attributions will be correct. Nevertheless, we are so addicted to attribution that it truly takes great discipline on our part even to practice such methods. No addict likes to delay gratification, and as attribution addicts none of us likes to wait patiently to make attributions only under optimal circumstances for avoiding errors. Even the most painstaking scholars and scientists have areas of life in which they must resist a strong natural inclination to jump to conclusions on inadequate data and by unsound means, and they often succumb despite their resistance.

In truth, we are all attribution addicts at least to some extent.

The Role of Attribution in Other Addictions

If full-blown addiction to attribution is not a universal human phenomenon, there is at least an addictive element in all human attribution, as the natural human resistance to scientific and scholarly methodology just mentioned shows. At the same time, attribution plays a role in the development and continuation of all other addictions. Thus, not only is attribution a root addiction of its own, but it is also at the root of the other addictions. In fact, without using the term, we have already touched more than once on the role that attribution plays in the genesis and maintenance of addiction.

At the very first stage of addiction, that of initial temptation towards addiction, potential addicts must attribute whatever effects they are feeling *to* the drug or other substance they are taking, or process in which they are engaging, at the time. Otherwise, addiction will not occur. It will have no foundation on which to build.

For example, if my friend who was once tempted to become addicted to heroin after smoking a small amount of it had not attributed what he was feeling to the heroin, he would never have experienced such a temptation. If he had attributed his sensations to some other source—perhaps to some personal success he had just experienced in his work or home life, or to some glandular malfunction—then heroin would have had no addictive appeal for him. It was only his attribution of those sensations to the drug that could *invest* heroin with such addictive potential.

Thus, attribution plays a vital role in the genesis of initial temptation toward addiction. Then, no sooner have addicts yielded to the temptation set up by their attributions of mood- or sensation-altering power to potentially addicting substances and processes, than attribution begins to play another, equally vital role—that uncovered in the research we have already mentioned concerning "expectancies." Having invested the objects of their addictions with psychoactive power by their initial attributions, addicts then persistently continue to attribute that same power to those objects in their subsequent experiences, even if the objective evidence of those subsequent experiences goes against that attribution. On the basis of such expectancies, addicts attribute to *themselves* recurrently positive experiences whenever they do practice the addiction. That is, the attributions constituting such expectancies begin to function as self-fulfilling prophecies. As addicts experience it *through* their own attributions, every time they practice their addictions the results on themselves are good. Then, on the rare occasions the contrary evidence is just too overwhelming, addicts are ready with a host of other attributions—namely, a host of explanations why "this time" there was something that got in the way of the regularly expected payoff.

It is also only thanks to attributions that discomfort associated with "withdrawal" can come to play a role in maintaining addiction. We recall William S. Burroughs' remark that narcotics addicts have to *learn* to associate the signs of their discomfort with having acquired a "habit." Of course, other, more experienced addicts are usually glad to assist as teachers. What they teach addicts is to associate the signs of discomfort with withdrawal, to attribute them to withdrawal as their cause.

Conversely, addicts in withdrawal attribute to the objects of their addictions the power to *relieve* them of their discomfort. They can then go on to attribute to themselves the pursuit of such relief as a motive for returning to "using." In turn, the very expectancies they effect in themselves by those attributions then set addicts up to *experience* tremendous relief if they do "pick up" again—which reinforces the expectancies involved, which reinforce the attributions of power to the objects of addiction, and so on, round and round the same circle over and over again. With each revolution, the existential equation of addiction etches itself more deeply in the addict's mind.

It is now time for us to consider how to break out of that circle, how to cancel that equation. It is time, that is, to consider how we should respond to addiction.

PART IV

RESPONDING
TO ADDICTION

·9·

"Right Effort" Towards Addiction

"Right Effort"

After his own enlightenment, the Buddha (which means "enlightened one" or "awakened one") taught that there is a way to spiritual liberation. That way is the "Noble Eightfold Path." In Buddhism, "right effort" is one of the eight constituents of that path. (The other seven are right understanding, right aspiration, right action, right speech, right livelihood, right meditation, and right mindfulness.)

To make the right effort is to develop effective or skillful ways of responding to experience in order to bring about liberation, and then to practice responding in those ways on a continuing basis until they become habitual. To put it in traditional Western language, right effort is a matter of building one's character. The person who practices right effort eventually acquires a set of solid dispositions to respond to experience in a liberating way. One then acts out of that acquired character, rather than on the basis of fleeting impressions. One is able to live life "deliberately" (to borrow a phrase from Thoreau), instead of being at the mercy of one's passing impulses.

Buddhist doctrine teaches that as part of the Noble Eightfold Path making right effort (developing a character for liberation) is itself, in turn, a fourfold process. It is here, above all, that we of the West can learn something from the East, which is of crucial importance for responding to addiction. The Western tendency is to see only part of what Buddha and his followers saw concerning right effort or character development.

Throughout the Western tradition, that process of developing character has been formulated in a predominantly *negative* way, as a matter of the observance of prohibitions and restrictions. All the way back at least to Socrates among the ancient Greeks, character formation has been conceived primarily in terms of avoiding doing anything wrong, rather than in terms of actively doing something right. Plato's *Apology,* for example, contains a famous passage in which Socrates discusses the "divine voice" that he sometimes hears speak to him inwardly. It is revealing that Socrates' voice speaks to him only when he is about to do something wrong. It warns him off from doing things, rather than calling upon him to perform positive actions. The voice always says "No," never "Yes."

Socrates' voice of divine warning later became the Western notion of "conscience." As traditionally conceived, our conscience is what keeps us from doing wrong. It warns us away from moral mistakes, telling us what *not* to do, but it doesn't tell us what we *should* do. In the Western tradition we are not given any assurance that following our conscience will lead us to do actual good. We are at most assured that if we heed Jiminy Cricket's admonition in Walt Disney's *Pinnochio* and always let our conscience be our guide, we will not do evil. Conscience, at least by tradition, will at most keep us away from vice; it won't show us how to acquire virtue.

In contrast, the Buddhist notion of right effort involves much more than merely avoiding vice. Buddhism gives equal importance to the other side of the avoidance of vice—namely, the acquisition of virtue. To be sure, right effort involves the avoidance of what is "bad," but only coupled with the cultivation of what is "good."

First of all, according to the Buddhists, it is not enough just to avoid committing wrongful acts. The best that the successful avoidance of wrongful acts will give us is a way to keep *new* vices from springing up in us.

That, of course, is important; and Buddhism clearly recognizes that it is. In fact, the idea that new vices do indeed spring up from wrongful acts is, if anything, even more entrenched in Eastern thought in general than it is in Western. The doctrine of *karma* sees to that. According to that doctrine, one can never escape the moral consequences of one's acts. Even death does not bring release from those consequences, since death is only the end of one reincarnation and the prelude to another, and the sort of rebirth one takes is an inescapable function of the *karma*, the sum total of moral assets and liabilities, that one has stored up in one's previous lives.

Thus, avoiding the acquisition of new vices (avoiding new negative *karma*) is an important part of right effort. However, it is only one part. There are three others.

If all we do is resist the formation of new vices, we will still remain victims of our *old* ones. Accordingly, besides avoiding the acquisition of additional undesirable traits we need to eliminate those we have already developed. That is the second part of right effort: uprooting the negative character traits that we already have (or that already have us).

However, in uprooting undesirable characteristics, care must be taken not to damage desirable ones in the process. As in gardening, we want to eliminate the weeds, not the vegetables or flowers. The third part of right effort consists of endeavoring to keep the desirable character traits or virtues we already have.

Finally, we don't just want to keep the good traits we already have. We also want to develop more good traits. Just as we want not only to avoid developing more bad habits, but also to eliminate our old ones, so do we want not only to keep our good habits, but also to acquire new ones. Thus, the fourth and final aspect of right effort is the formation of new positive characteristics or virtues.

Right effort, then, is the fourfold endeavor to keep all the good traits we already have while developing more, at the same time eliminating our bad traits while not developing more. Such an effort is precisely what we must make if we are ever adequately to respond to addiction. We must couple a deliberate, strong resistance to new temptations toward addiction with an equally deliberate and strong attempt to overcome whatever addictions are already present. At the same time, we must combine that effort against addiction with an opposite but equal effort to retain whatever we already have that fills in a positive way the longings that underlie addiction. Nor is it enough just to cultivate the positive elements already present. We must also go on to develop new ones.

If it is to be successful, this fourfold approach cannot be pieced together ad hoc. We cannot simply work on each of the four elements independently of one another, and then glue them together in hopes of coming up with an effective response to addiction. Instead, the four elements must be developed together, in a single unified and unifying spirit of a completely *positive* nature. That is, even the two apparently "negative" moments (avoiding new addictions and uprooting old ones) must be pursued in a way that reveals a hidden "positive" undercurrent. If they are allowed to remain negative, those two will pollute the whole response to addiction, shooting it all through with negativity. What started out to become right effort toward addiction will become, instead, just another addictive perversion.

We consider each of the four parts of genuine right effort toward addiction in turn, paying special attention to the way in which even avoiding and uprooting addiction can be transformed from something negative into something positive.

Don't Just Say No

In his award-winning book on Gandhi, the developmental psychologist Erik H. Erikson makes an interesting remark concerning Gandhi's years as a young man studying in England to become a lawyer. The context for the remark is a discussion of Gandhi's struggles to honor an oath he made to to his mother before he left India. Gandhi had vowed to his mother that while he was in England he would maintain the vegetarianism that is a traditional part of the Hindu-Jain religious background into which Gandhi was born. Erikson comments that the future apostle of nonviolence, who would eventually lead India to independence from British rule and inspire generations of future nonviolent social activists, had to learn an important lesson through those youthful struggles with a vegetarian diet in the land of beef and mutton. As Erikson puts it, Gandhi "had to learn to *choose actively and affirmatively what not to do—* an ethical capacity not to be confused with the moralistic inability to break a prohibition."[1]

The same kind of active, affirmative choice of "what not to do" that belongs to vegetarianism in cases such as Gandhi's is also involved in cases of the genuine call to celibacy, such as have occurred throughout history in numerous religions. That includes Christianity, where celibacy belongs not only to the Roman Catholic priesthood but also to Christian monasticism in general (and beyond). If one is to maintain a vow of celibacy without becoming emotionally and sexually disabled, one must learn the same lesson Gandhi did for vegetarianism. If one cannot learn to embrace celibacy as a healthy, joyous expression of one's very sexuality, then one is destined either to abandon one's vow or to become the sort of distorted personality in whom obsessive lasciviousness disguises itself as hypocritical righteousness. Unfortunately, the history of Christianity is all too full of examples of just how perverted monks and priests can become, if they cannot succeed in transforming their celibacy (on the surface, a matter of *refraining* from something—namely from genital sexual activity) into something wholly *positive.*

The same thing applies to refraining from addictive pursuits, that is, to rejecting the temptations of addiction, temptations to become addicted. The person who cannot pass beyond merely resisting temptation, replacing mere resistance with something positive, will not escape addiction. Such persons will no more escape addiction than the priest who fondles children or devotes hours to his private collection of pornography has escaped lust. At most, they will manage to avoid a given addiction. My friend who once smoked heroin, and then swore off it forever because he found it so tempting, provides an example of how mere resistance can allow that much. However, escaping one addiction is not escaping addiction in general. The person who avoids becoming addicted to heroin can still become addicted to other things—and will, if the avoidance remains nothing but a negative reaction to specific temptations. The only proof against addiction in general is the sort of active and affirmative choice of "what not to do" that Erikson mentions, the sort of choice involved in Gandhi's vegetarianism or genuine calls to celibacy.

Nietzsche has his Zarathustra deride those who think themselves good, just because they have no claws. Nietzsche thereby echoes a sentiment of Shakespeare, who in one of his sonnets praises those who have the power to hurt others, but refrain from it, as opposed to those who refrain from hurting others only because they couldn't even if they wanted to, or who are afraid of the consequences. The fear of hell will not, alone, get one into heaven, nor can the person who never experiences temptation in the first place take credit for not yielding to it.

The general term for refraining from some common practice or pursuit is *abstinence*. The vegetarian practices abstinence from eating meat. The celibate practices abstinence from genital sexual acts. One who refrains from something to which one is tempted to become addicted practices abstinence from that thing.

A person who was never tempted to use heroin could not properly be said to "abstain" from using it. Not using heroin would require no effort on that person's part. In the same way, those who don't drink simply because they never acquired the taste for alcohol don't abstain from it. Once again, there is no self-restraint involved. We are dealing with abstinence in the proper sense only where self-restraint is required.

What allows us to transform abstinence (whether from meat, from genital sex, from heroin, from child molestation, or whatever) from negative *avoidance* into positive *embrace* is this element of self-restraint at the heart of all abstinence. If we abstain from doing something merely because we fear the consequences of doing it, either on practical or on moral grounds (as with Erikson's "moralistic inability to break a prohibition," which, incidentally, easily becomes what Gerald May calls an "aversive addiction"), then we remain at the level of negative avoidance. However, once we begin to abstain from something *for the sake of exercising our own self-restraint*, we pass over from a negative abstinence to a positive one. From that point on, abstaining becomes its own, ever-growing reward.

It is the same with the exercise of self-restraint as it is with physical exercise. If we engage in physical activity solely to avoid ill health, we soon tire of it. If we don't abandon it after an initial period of resolution, we stick to our exercise regime only grudgingly and with mounting difficulty. We are, in fact, probably doing ourselves more harm than good, since our stress level is bound to rise under such circumstances. On the other hand, if we once get to the point of enjoying the physical activity for its own sake, and not merely as a means to lessen the risks to our health, we will be able to continue regular exercise indefinitely. All other things being equal, it will become easier and easier for us to exercise, rather than harder and harder—and the benefits to our health will accrue naturally.

That is also how it is with abstinence. Our chances of continuing to abstain—especially our chances of continuing to do so without falling prey to emotional and psychological problems—are low, if the only motivation we can muster for abstaining is avoiding the risk of addiction. Yet by embracing abstinence as a natural way of exercising, and thereby growing in, self-restraint, we will find ourselves increasingly able to abstain, while avoiding addiction just takes care of itself.

American public policy toward addiction, whether at the national, state, or local level, is almost exclusively concerned with the purely negative enterprise of resisting addiction. Throughout the history of American governmental concern with addiction, the focus has been upon the interdiction of substances for which American society shows significant rates of addiction. The issue of reducing rates of addiction has been seen in terms of "cutting off the supply." In the more recent past, attempts at interdiction of controlled substances have been coupled with a youth-oriented, media-intensive public campaign of education concerning drugs, and the refrain that youth should "Just say no" to them.

However effective such approaches may be in the short run or with regard to specific addictions (and even that remains in dispute), they do nothing to address the underlying problem of addiction in general. It is certainly not implausible to suggest that addiction, say, to jogging, is preferable to addiction to hard drugs; but the point that must be made is that *no* addiction is ultimately desirable. What is more, intense negative focus upon avoiding addiction by controlling supply inevitably tends to exacerbate the very thing it is designed to avoid. At the individual level, the more one concentrates exclusively on avoiding a given addiction, the more obsessively one keeps one's attention riveted on the potential object of that addiction. But obsessive preoccupation with something is precisely what addiction is. Addicts who must expend all their energy *avoiding* drugs are no less hooked than those who do drugs constantly.

At the institutional level, large-scale attempts to control addiction through interdiction, education, and admonishment require the institutionalization of the means necessary to carry them out.

The natural result is that those who are given responsibility for applying those means come to have a vested, albeit for the most part hidden and unintentional, interest in *fostering* the very thing they are ostensibly dedicated to eradicating. Bureaucrats whose salaries will continue only so long as there is a high enough rate of addiction in our society to justify those salaries will have an interest, even despite themselves, in seeing to it that the rate of addiction does not fall too dramatically. (William S. Burroughs' *Naked Lunch* is a brilliant, and brutally honest, depiction of just that phenomenon.)

Social theorist and activist Ivan Illich has documented the danger of institutions that grow beyond a certain point becoming "specifically counterproductive"—that is, of institutions coming actually to serve a purpose exactly opposite to that for which they were initially created.[2] This is precisely the danger with the sorts of negative governmental policies toward addiction that we are discussing. Designed to lessen addiction, all too easily they end up increasing it.

If we, either as individuals or as a society, are to respond to addiction with "right effort," we must transcend such negative approaches. We must learn Gandhi's lesson.

"You Never Have to Take Another Drink Again"

At some point during their first meeting, newcomers to Alcoholics Anonymous are often told: "You never have to take another drink again as long as you live, if you don't want to." To alcoholics who have hit bottom and are in the right place to hear it, that is a message of astonishing liberation. Practicing alcoholics are precisely individuals who experience themselves as "having" to drink: Their very lives and identities are wrapped up in their drinking. For such alcoholics to go into an AA meeting and be told they never have to take another drink again—and to *believe* what they have just been told—brings overwhelming relief. It literally changes their entire lives.

Of course, newcomers who do *not* believe this message will not be changed by it. Accordingly, the crucial question is what circumstances are most conducive to such belief. If we are to make the right effort in response to addiction, then we need an answer to that question. In addition to knowing how to foster the avoidance of addiction in the first place (what we just discussed in the preceding section of this chapter), we need to know how to help those who are already addicted become liberated from their addictions. We need to know how best to bring them the liberating word—the word that frees them from their addictive bondage.

Alcoholics Anonymous, where so many alcoholics have actually heard just such a word liberating them from dependence on alcohol, can teach us a great deal along those lines. Part of what it has to teach has already been widely learned. We touched on it a moment ago. Addicts themselves must be *ready* to hear the liberating word; they must have developed ears to hear it.

Addicts are made ready by "hitting bottom." That is why successful "intervention" strategies attempt to "raise the bottom" by confronting addicts with the consequences of their addictions. It is also why right effort toward addiction on the part of those of us who have relationships with addicts requires that we stop "enabling" the addicts in our lives. To do that, we must first become *aware* of how we enable (that is, as we discussed earlier, how we actually *dis*able, all the while under the intention of helping) the addicts with whom we have relationships. On our part that requires careful, strenuous reflection on our own behavior, on an ongoing basis. Then, we must go on to *change* how we act. We must carry the results of our self-scrutiny over into action, so that we can *stop* doing things that enable addiction.

The same thing applies at the level of society and its institutions. Right effort toward addiction at the social or governmental level also requires careful, deliberate study of the ways in which institutional and governmental policies, as well as customs and manners and all the other things that structure social life in general, play an enabling role for addiction. Then it requires concerted, sustained attempts to change those policies, and the like, so that they no longer enable (= disable) the addicts among us.

So far, only the barest beginning has been made to discover what needs to be changed, let alone actually to effect the necessary changes. Every institution of society needs to be subjected to a careful critique along those very lines,[3] if we are really serious about overcoming addiction. Each of us individually should also spend time thinking about how our own professions, and our own ways of working within them, foster addiction. (Most or all professions do foster addiction, and academic philosophy is most definitely *not* an exception.)

In sum, to help addicts grow ears to hear the word that can liberate them from their addictions, we, both individually and collectively, need *actively to let them hit bottom*. However, that is only one half of what is necessary. The other half consists of finding the right spokespersons to deliver the liberating word. Put differently, we need to find a way to deliver that word *with authority*—an authority that will be acknowledged by the addicts themselves. It is only coming from the right mouth that any word can liberate.

When a newcomer who has hit bottom goes to an AA meeting and listens to what is said, he or she can hear that those who are speaking know what they are talking about. They have an authority established on the most solid credentials, namely, the credentials of their own experiences. A lifelong teetotaler telling alcoholics they never have to drink again, if they don't want to, doesn't have any standing to make what is said heard. What does a teetotaler know about it? Nothing, at least so far as an alcoholic is concerned. However, as the book *Alcoholics Anonymous* says, another alcoholic, someone who has been through the same experience, and who doesn't preach or scold, but simply shares his or her own story, can soon gain the confidence of even the most cynical fellow alcoholic—at least with regard to the business of alcohol and alcoholism.

What allows AA newcomers who have truly hit bottom to be suddenly, miraculously liberated simply by being told that they never have to take another drink again is who is doing the telling. Because those who deliver that message can do so with an authority the newcomer can acknowledge, that newcomer can come to *believe* it in the deepest, most effective sense.

Uprooting an addiction after it has already taken hold is a very different thing from avoiding becoming addicted in the first place. Embracing and nurturing self-restraint as a positive value can keep addiction from taking root, but once addiction has put down roots that approach is no longer effective. For example, it doesn't do much good to tell someone who smokes a minimum of three packs of cigarettes a day to exercise self-restraint. That person's capacity for self-restraint toward smoking has long since been lost completely.

When addiction is already present, only some sort of experience of being *liberated* from the addiction will allow the addict truly to overcome it (as opposed, say, to just substituting one addiction for another). Someone must deliver to the addict the message of liberation. Someone with authority to do so must say the liberating word. The experience of self-restraint is the positive underpinning of the apparently wholly negative task of avoiding initial addiction. Similarly, the experience of being freed by having such a word spoken to one is the underlying positive phenomenon that makes the apparently wholly negative task of overcoming an already present addiction possible.

What such freeing words do is to *allow* addicts to give up their addictions. These words give addicts *permission* not to practice their addictions any longer. Such permission is what first of all clears the way of recovery. It is what first of all makes it possible for addicts to do what they need to do in their own lives in order to free themselves from addictive dependency and remain free of it.

If we can speak with authority on the basis of our own experience of recovery from addiction, then right effort requires us actually to speak words of liberation to those who are still in bondage. Liberated addicts must tell other addicts what they themselves were once told, just as AA's twelfth step requires that alcoholics who have themselves had a "spiritual awakening" as a result of taking the preceding eleven steps must try to "carry the message to the alcoholic who still suffers."

To the extent that we are not addicts, and therefore lack the authority to speak words of liberation ourselves, right effort requires us to become aware of how we enable addiction, and to work at stopping it. However, in the same way that avoiding addiction cannot succeed if approached solely in negative terms, stopping enabling ultimately involves committing ourselves to something positive. It involves *actively granting* addicts, who are already in recovery or not yet there, the right to live out their own lives and to make their own choices as they see fit, either in favor of recovery or against it, rather than persisting in the unconscious endeavor to *manipulate* them into recovering. Thus, truly to stop enabling is not just to stop enabling. It is to begin *empowering*.

Finally, to the extent that we are still practicing addicts ourselves, we must wait upon the freeing word.

". . . In All Our Affairs"

After warning alcoholics who have taken the first eleven steps that they need to try to give other alcoholics what they have been given, AA's twelfth step ends by admonishing them to continue practicing the principles which are embodied ˙ ᴉ all Twelve Steps. In fact, according to step twelve, they must practice those principles in *all* their affairs.

That is an excellent prescription for retaining the good traits that one has already acquired by that point in one's recovery. Not only does practice make perfect, as an old proverb has it. It is also the case that we lose what we don't use, as a more recent one tells us.

The third part of right effort is to retain the good characteristics one already has. The only reliable way to do that is to follow AA's advice and to practice using those characteristics whenever the opportunity to do so presents itself. That is, it is to do the very things those characteristics dispose us to do whenever we can. That way, we not only assure that we will not lose them through disuse, but we also strengthen them further. That, in turn, provides us with ever greater protection against encroachments on the part of our vices. Here, at least, the best defense is a good offense.

Our discussion of this aspect of right effort toward addiction can be quite brief. Right effort toward addiction demands of all of us, whether addicts or not and whether individually or collectively, that we actively exercise our virtues whenever and wherever possible. It requires that we try to act well in all our affairs. In that regard, however, no distinction can be drawn between right effort towards addiction and right effort in general. None of us, whether addicts or nonaddicts, whether taken as individuals or taken collectively, should do less.

Lest that seem too harsh, let us note that, again as with physical exercise, the exercise of virtue becomes easier the more we do it. At the beginning it requires much exertion on our part, and rigorous self-scrutiny. Eventually, however, we find ourselves effortlessly doing what we used to accomplish only with great effort. It is just as St. Benedict says in the Prologue to his *Rule*, in discussing the rigors of monastic life. "Do not be daunted immediately by fear and run away from the road that leads to salvation," he encourages the reader. "It is bound to be narrow at the outset. But as we progress in this way of life and in faith, we shall run on the path of God's commandments, our hearts overflowing with the inexpressible delight of love."[4]

"A Substitute, and Vastly More"

The last of the four parts of right effort demands that we try to acquire new virtues, not just rest content with the ones we already have. Indeed, if all we do is try to retain our old virtues, we will soon find that even they will slip away, to be replaced by vices. It is the same with virtues as it is with living things: They are always either growing or decaying; they are never just holding their own.

Nor is it only in order to keep the good traits we already have that we must cultivate more. The authors of *Alcoholics Anonymous* assure alcoholics that in order to stop drinking they must find a "substitute" for alcohol. The same passage goes on to assure them that there is indeed a substitute—"a substitute, and vastly more."[5] In truth, only a substitute that is vastly more than any mere substitute could possibly give addicts what they need to recover fully from addiction (to become "happy, respected, and useful once more"[6]). Anything that lets addicts do no more than stop practicing their given addictions would not really let them overcome addiction at all. At most, it would simply replace one addiction with another (one less harmful, it is to be hoped).

For example, if all that the newly formed AA had offered to newcomers in the 1930s had been a way to stop drinking, while leaving everything else in their lives the same, AA would never have gotten off the ground. What alcoholic would be interested in such a proposition? Just to stop drinking, without doing anything to address the underlying issues (the ones that drinking itself addresses for an alcoholic, in however illusory a fashion), would only leave a vacuum that other addictions would be waiting to fill.

If all that we do is offer addicts, whether ourselves or others, a way to stop "practicing" or "using," it is no wonder that addicts remain unmoved. Suppose we go further and tack on a way for addicts also to avoid forming new addictions, while they are kicking their old habits. Imagine that, as a final inducement, we even throw in a way for them to keep all the good, healthy, nonaddictive elements they already have in themselves and their lives. Even then, our offer will leave the vast majority of addicts cold.

That is because, in the final analysis, such an offer can be of no more than *negative* interest. It is at most a matter of negative, rather than positive, reinforcement. At most, it recommends itself as a way for addicts to unburden themselves of all the undesirable consequences of their addictive behaviors, at no long-term expense to themselves.

At first glance, the prospect of abandoning addictive behaviors without developing new ones and without sacrificing anything of lasting value looks like quite a bargain. However, reflection shows that such a prospect would really have only limited appeal. It would only recommend itself to those for whom the current negative consequences of their addictions are unpleasant enough to make avoiding those consequences more important than attaining whatever positive satisfaction continued practice of the addiction promises to give them.

Any addict can tell us how long such negative motivation lasts. It lasts only as long as the memory of the undesirable consequences stays strong. But the more successful one is at avoiding an addictive practice on the grounds of such motivation, the less strong does that very memory become. Before long, the memory of the pain that one brought on oneself through the addiction begins to pale in comparison to the anticipation of the satisfaction that would immediately attend relapse into the addiction. Sometimes in AA it is said that the farther away one is from one's last drink, the closer one is to the next one. That is surely true for alcoholics and all other addicts whose only reason to stop "using" is to avoid negative consequences that accompany continuing usage.

To broaden a line from "The Doctor's Opinion" in *Alcoholics Anonymous* that we have heard before, addicts are all restless, irritable, and discontented, unless they can again experience the sense of ease and comfort that comes at once from returning to the addictive practice. If the results of that practice become difficult enough, addicts can for a time give up their addictions. But that does not mean they can give up being restless, irritable, and discontented. Once they stop practicing their addictions, they begin escaping the negative consequences of those addictions, of course. For that very reason, however, the restlessness, irritability, and discontent that they continue to experience simultaneously begin to make the addictive practice look all the more desirable again.

That condition of restlessness, irritability, and discontent is not ultimately dependent upon external circumstances. Instead, in accordance with the existential nature and spiritual meaning of addiction, it is inseparable from addicts' own basic sense of themselves. It constitutes an addict's fundamental and continual experiential condition. Accordingly, it cannot be assuaged on any lasting basis by changes in the external circumstances of an addict's life, including those very changes for the good that are brought about by the cessation of the addictive behavior.

To escape addiction, addicts must have "something more." There must be a complete shift of focus from the negative avoidance of what is perceived as undesirable to the positive pursuit of something—something that is perceived as *more* desirable than the addiction itself.

At least to addicts who have experienced the "spiritual awakening" referred to in AA's step twelve, the continued effort to develop one's positive traits ever more fully, and to acquire ever more positive traits (all conceived as surrender to a "higher power"), offers that "something more." The commitment to "progress, not perfection" becomes a substitute for the addiction—a substitute, and vastly more.

Precisely because the idea of progress, unlike that of perfection, is in principle open-ended (that is, there is no limit built into the idea of possible progress or positive development as such), it provides addicts with a focus on *process*, rather than *results*. Accordingly, it offers the same sort of *immediate gratification* that the addictive practice itself used to provide. If one's sense of satisfaction derives from how doggedly one is trudging along "the Road to Happy Destiny" (as it is called at one point in *Alcoholics Anonymous*)[7], rather than from having arrived at the end of that road, then one doesn't have to wait to get to some destination before one begins to enjoy oneself.

The planting and nurturing of ever more good traits—the fourth part of right effort—does more than merely provide a substitute for addiction. It provides vastly more than that. Finally, without that "vastly more," there really is no substitute for addiction. And if there is no substitute for addiction, there is also no avoiding it, no overcoming it, and no preserving of anything against it—the first three parts of right effort.

Just saying no is never enough, not even for just saying no.

·10·

Freedom from Addiction:
The Nonaddictive Mind

Discussing how AA works, David Berenson, an expert on alcoholism and recovery from it, makes this remark: "AA is designed so that a person can stop drinking by either education, therapeutic change, or transformation." Those who belong to the first group only need to be given information in order to quit—the sort of information they can pick up easily by attending a few AA meetings. In contrast, members of the second group must undergo a "second order change similar to changes brought about in therapy" in order to stop drinking. Finally, those who belong to the third group are men and women brought to abandon drinking through "a full-fledged transformative shift or real religious insight."[1]

The first group, those who only need to be given the right information in order to quit drinking, make up only a small percentage of those for whom AA provides a solution to their drinking problems, Berenson says. That is readily understandable. Someone who could quit drinking so easily is unlikely to have gone very far down the road of alcohol addiction in the first place. However, it is rare for anyone who has not traveled a sizeable stretch of that road to find his or her way into an AA meeting. Although it contains a tip of the hat to those who can so easily do a "right about-face" in their drinking, it is not primarily for such persons that *Alcoholics Anonymous* was written.[2]

Those in Berenson's second group are individuals who cannot

simply stop drinking, without addressing the underlying conditions within themselves that foster their alcoholism. That is what Berenson means by speaking of the need for a "second order change" in such cases. These drinkers are those who have made various attempts to stop drinking, using various means, but to no avail. Like the yo-yo dieter who can take pounds off, but can't keep them off, such drinkers go through periods in which they refrain from drinking, but they find themselves unable to sustain their sobriety. What these overeaters and drinkers both must finally do if they are to break out of that circle is to shift their attention from the habit they are trying to break (overeating or drinking—the level of "first order change") to focus on what lies beneath that habit and supports it (the level of "second order change"). According to Berenson, those who belong to this group constitute the majority of those who succeed in quitting drinking through AA.

Berenson says that those in the final group, who are brought to quit drinking through a complete spiritual transformation, make up only a distinct minority of AA's membership. He may be right. Nevertheless, it is primarily to these drinkers that the book *Alcoholics Anonymous* is addressed, and it was drinkers of that type who wrote and edited it in the first place. Although that group of original AA members went out of its way, in the final, published version of the book, to leave open the question of what road one had to travel to reach the desired goal (what idea of God one needed, for example), they left no uncertainty at all when it came to defining that goal itself. The goal was nothing short of the complete transformation or conversion at issue in Berenson's third category.

As those early AA members understood, genuine freedom from addiction—not just freedom from *an* addiction, but freedom from addiction as such—requires no less.

Changing Masters

Some smokers can quit smoking by chewing gum incessantly. The gum chewing becomes a replacement for the smoking. It becomes a substitute (though not more than a substitute—as I can personally testify, it is at best only a partial replacement and a third-rate one at that). In the same way, one common treatment for heroin addiction replaces heroin with another drug, methadone.

In turn, AA meetings are notorious for being smoke filled, even in this day of rising antismoking sentiment. Many newcomers to AA who are smokers find their cigarette consumption rising during the early stages of their sobriety. AA members also drink inordinately large amounts of coffee, not only at meetings but also in smaller groups of two or more that form before and after meetings, or as the result of planned or unplanned get-togethers apart from formal AA meetings.

Finally, anyone who spends much time around AA or any of its various spinoff Twelve Step groups may soon begin to see some grounds for a complaint that is sometimes lodged against the AA approach. The complaint is that it is only by devoting themselves obsessively to AA (by going to meeting after meeting, socializing only with other AA members, and, in short, coming to center their whole lives around AA functions) that alcoholics in AA manage to give up their drinking. They give up alcohol only by becoming AA junkies, as it were. That is, they really only substitute one addiction for another.

That can happen. It does happen in some cases. When it does, it is an interesting example of what is called "cross-addiction." Cross-addiction is the phenomenon in which someone addicted to one thing is readily able to shift over to another thing, whenever access to the first thing is blocked. If access to the addictive object of first choice is blocked through the loss of a connection, intense family pressure, or some other source, a person who is cross-addicted will be able to transfer his or her addiction to some substitute with little or no experiential distress. So, for example, someone who is addicted to marijuana but also cross-addicted to alcohol will prefer marijuana over alcohol, but will easily be able to shift over to alcohol if the supply of marijuana gets cut off.

Even more common than cross-addiction is multiple addiction, in which one is addicted to more than one thing. Many alcoholics are also addicted to nicotine and caffeine, for example. In fact, those who are addicted to only one thing are probably quite rare. This would conform to the existential nature of addiction and the fact that addiction *to being addicted* plays a role in all addiction to specific objects, as we have remarked before.

The cross-addict can escape bondage to the object of addiction by shifting to the object of cross-addiction. The multiple addict can use his or her other addictions to help break the one addictive practice that is proving to be the most troublesome. By relying more heavily on cigarettes and coffee to get one through the day, for instance, an alcoholic may be able to stay away from alcohol—especially if the alcoholic has a third or even fourth addiction to indulge for relief from the existential pain of going without a drink. To give another, related example, many AA members have found themselves gaining weight at an alarming rate once they stopped drinking. In many such cases, what is involved is the substitution of an addictive relationship to food for an addictive relationship to alcohol.

Depending on the perspective we adopt, some addictions can appear worse than others. For example, smoking is undeniably a life-threatening addiction. It threatens both the life of the smoker and the lives of nonsmokers who are exposed to the smoke. But it does not have as markedly corrosive an effect on the fabric of the lives it threatens as does alcohol. For one thing, the effects of nicotine do not lead to the sorts of wholesale personality and behavioral changes that can often accompany alcohol intoxication.

To take another example, overuse of caffeine is clearly not as directly and immediately life threatening as smoking. Nor does it have any negative physical effects on those who are in the vicinity of the coffee or tea drinker when the latter is "using." The scent of coffee or tea is not noxious, as is that of burning cigarettes to most nonsmokers; and there is no social stigma currently attached to drinking either of those two beverages.

Accordingly, at least at one level the attitude expressed at one point in *Alcoholics Anonymous* makes very good sense. That is the attitude that it is better not to worry about such things as smoking or drinking too much coffee, if smoking and coffee drinking help an alcoholic stay away from alcohol. "First things first," is the advice given there,[3] and echoed at AA meetings. Newcomers to AA who smoke are often advised not even to try quitting smoking until they have made it through at least one year without drinking any alcohol.

Nevertheless, at another level the truth of the matter is still that to exchange one object of addiction for another is merely to change masters, regardless of how mild one's new master may be in comparison to the old. It is also still true that to be addicted is always to be enslaved to *some* master, regardless of the accompanying effects of that enslavement on oneself or others. For that reason, it is understandable that at least one well-known alcoholism counselor and author requires his alcoholic-potential clients (and their families as well) to promise to give up both nicotine and caffeine as well as alcohol, before he will take them on.[4] On similar grounds, many alcoholism rehabilitation and treatment centers serve only decaffeinated coffee in their facilities.

For those who are ready for it, such a simultaneous frontal assault on all of one's addictions at once might even strengthen their motivation. Nevertheless, just as cross-addicts have a preferred addiction, so do multiple addicts have a primary addiction, the one that causes the most trouble in their lives. Although freedom from addiction as such should be the ultimate goal, AA is surely right in thinking that not all addictions are equally destructive—at least not at a given time in the addict's life, corresponding to uneven stages of development in the addict's various addictions. Furthermore, those who have hit bottom with one of their addictions may not yet have done so with regard to all of them. If so, they might be scared off by the demand to go cold turkey on everything at once. For example, an alcoholic who has reached the point of finally being willing to do what is necessary to stop drinking may balk at giving up smoking at the same time. Such a requirement could provide the part of the alcoholic's mind that is still uncertain about quitting drinking (and there is always such a part in an alcoholic's mind) with an excuse not to do so.

The best approach would therefore seem to be to make a realistic assessment of each individual case, and then to do what seems best for that particular situation. What is of crucial importance, however, is that the *ultimate goal* remain the same, and that whatever approach is adopted be chosen as the best available means for reaching it. That ultimate goal should be *freedom from addiction as such*, as opposed to freedom merely from any specific addiction. In a given case, changing masters may be the most that can be hoped for in the short term. Sometimes, a change of masters can bring a slave closer to the day of being set free from slavery; sometimes not. If such an exchange can hasten that day, an unrealistic insistence on complete freedom right now will only postpone it indefinitely. An all-or-nothing approach is one of the characteristics of addictive thinking.

To reach the ultimate goal of freedom from all addiction, one must begin where one is, rather than daydreaming about being elsewhere. One can be set free from addiction in general only by being set free from all of one's specific addictions. If some addicts find it reasonably possible to give up all their addictions at once, then they should probably do so. Others, however, may need to take them one at a time, as they grow in their ability to acknowledge and respond to them.

In fact, given the self-dissembling nature of addiction as such, it is no easy matter to become truly *aware* that one is addicted in the first place. "There is a difference between knowledge and awareness," writes Anthony de Mello, a Jesuit priest assigned to India and widely known in both the English- and the Spanish-speaking world for his writing and the retreats which he conducted until his sudden death in 1987.[5] De Mello's distinction can be usefully applied in the discussion of addiction. Many addicts may "know" that they are addicts. That is, they will assent to the proposition that they are addicted, perhaps even proclaiming it themselves while they pick up the next drink, snort the next line, and so on. But truly to become *aware* of their addiction is to reach the point at which such knowledge becomes internalized and lived out in their own experience. It is only at that point that they are at AA's first step toward freedom from addiction, the step of truly admitting one's powerlessness over the object of addiction, rather than just giving perfunctory, notional assent to the abstract idea of being powerless.

"A Position of Neutrality": Defining Abstinence

When it does come time to deal with a specific addiction, we need to distinguish between different types of addiction, with correspondingly different paths to freedom from them. One major distinction is between addictions to things we can learn to do without, and addictions to things we cannot learn to do without. Addictions to alcohol, nicotine, caffeine, narcotics, and other drugs are examples of the first type. Addiction to food is the most obvious example of the second type.

In the first case, one can go "cold turkey," and one can live the rest of one's life without ever taking any more of the substance, or engaging any more in the process, to which one is addicted. Hard as it may be for an alcoholic to imagine in the first few days of sobriety, it is possible to live a very full, rich, long, and rewarding life without ever taking any alcoholic drink. Smokers who quit smoking can quit completely, and never again light up a cigarette— or cigar or pipe, or pick up a plug of chewing tobacco, or in any other way go back to using nicotine. Drug addicts can get "clean," and then remain that way for the rest of their lives, however long those lives may prove to be.

However, going cold turkey on food, and then never eating again, is hardly a solution to food addiction. (Though it may provide a Swiftian solution to overpopulation.)

Sex addiction is an interesting example of an intermediate case between those two extremes. Examples throughout history of men and women who have maintained strict, lifelong celibacy prove that it is possible to learn to do without genital sex altogether. Nevertheless, it is only at great effort and very much against the natural human grain that anyone learns to do without it. As admirable as a life of chosen celibacy may be, it is not the only admirable way of living out one's sexual being. Nor is it required in order to free oneself from addiction to sex.

Thus, in cases such as food addiction, addicts cannot do altogether without the object of their addiction; in cases such as sex addiction it is unreasonable to demand addicts to do altogether without it. Accordingly, freedom from such addictions involves learning a new way of relating to the objects at issue, rather than learning to refrain from them entirely. What is more, for many years the possibility has been debated that something similar might also work even for alcoholics or drug addicts. That is, the question has repeatedly been raised whether alcoholics and drug addicts might not, with proper training, also learn how to continue using alcohol or drugs, but to use them nonaddictively.

That possibility has been most debated in the case of alcoholics. There, the standard way of putting the question is to ask whether alcoholics can be taught "controlled drinking," as opposed to "abstinence." That very way of putting it may distort the discussion, however. What is really at issue might better be formulated as a debate about what *constitutes* "abstinence" in such cases. That is, it is a matter of determining what *criteria* for abstinence are most appropriate.

George Vaillant makes the penetrating observation that problem drinkers who *do* eventually return to drinking after an initial period of abstinence, but who manage to avoid the recurrence of problems in connection with their drinking, do indeed have to practice *controlled* drinking. That is, they have to monitor their consumption carefully, and stop as soon as they begin to see warning signs of an impending relapse into their old problematic drinking behavior. They never, Vaillant's research shows, come to the point of relating to alcohol the way that those who have never had a problem with drinking relate to it naturally.[6] Such nonproblematic drinkers do not have to keep watch over their drinking, at least not on any regular basis. Instead, for the most part they can simply drink when and what they want. We might say that they are completely "free" drinkers, as opposed to "controlled" drinkers. They just don't have to worry about their alcohol consumption, one way or the other.

That observation also provides the key to formulating a clear definition of what constitutes freedom from any given addiction. Truly to be free from a given addiction is *no longer to have to worry about it*. In different terms, that is also precisely what is said about freedom from alcoholism in *Alcoholics Anonymous*. According to that source, alcoholics who genuinely commit themselves to taking the Twelve Steps eventually arrive at "a position of neutrality" towards alcohol. "We have not even sworn off," the passage continues. "Instead, the problem has been removed. It does not exist for us."[7]

No better definition of freedom from alcoholism could be imagined. For anyone who has ever been addicted to alcohol, truly to be free of that addiction is to reach just such a point of neutrality. It is to reach a point at which one no longer needs to avoid places where liquor is served, occasions when it is readily available, or company that enjoys drinking it. It is a point at which one no longer needs to watch over oneself carefully, looking concernedly for signs of a pending relapse into drinking. For any alcoholic who reaches such a point, alcohol has lost its power. For that very reason, such an alcoholic will "seldom be interested in liquor" and rarely even tempted to pick up a drink. On those rare occasions when temptation does occur, one will "recoil from it as from a hot flame."[8]

The same thing applies to any specific addiction. For someone suffering from that addiction to become free of it is for that person to arrive at "a position of neutrality" toward the object of the addiction. If one *has* arrived at such a point, then one will no longer need to worry about "controlling" one's access to the object of one's addiction. One will simply avail oneself of that object, or refrain from availing oneself of it, as need and circumstance dictate.

Alcohol is not something that we need in order to survive, as is the case with food. Nor is it even something that, although not absolutely essential for survival, is still so naturally important to us that there is something rare and heroic about being able to do without it, as is the case with sex. Accordingly, it is at least difficult to imagine a situation in which someone who has really attained freedom from an earlier addiction to alcohol would have good enough reason ever to take another drink. Why should one even bother, if the problem with alcohol truly has been removed? What could make it worth the risk of giving alcohol even a remote chance of reestablishing its power over one? For an alcoholic to take a drink after appearing to win victory over alcohol would at first glance be evidence that the victory was merely apparent, and that the addiction was really still quite active.

The term *abstinence* remains the best term we have for identifying the general goal of recovery from addiction. However, we must be careful to define it properly, if it is to serve that purpose well. To do that we must avoid defining abstinence in terms of refraining from *all* usage of the given object of addiction, without further qualification. Instead, we must define abstinence as refraining from all *addictive* usage of that object. To recover from addiction one must abstain from addictive usage of the object of one's addiction, not necessarily from all usage as such.

In some cases, to be sure, the most reasonable criterion to use for determining whether someone is truly "abstinent" with regard to a given addiction will be total nonusage. For the reasons just given, that criterion applies to alcoholism and similar addictions. In such cases the best criterion for "abstinence" is *no usage at all.*

On the other hand, because food *is* necessary for life itself, complete freedom from addiction to food means being able to eat naturally, when and as much as one likes, without constantly having to count calories or the like. Similarly, freedom from sex addiction means being able to have sex naturally, knowing that one can do so without risk of lapsing back into compulsive acting out. In those cases, coming up with a workable criterion for determining whether a recovering addict is maintaining abstinence is much more difficult than in cases such as alcoholism.

It is also that much more difficult to free oneself from such addictions—those to which the simple "no usage" criterion is not applicable. As criteria for success become less definite, failure becomes more common. The goal can still be stated clearly, however, even if the criterion for having arrived at that goal remains unstable. The goal—freedom from addiction, for any addiction whatever—is to reach a "position of neutrality" towards the object of the addiction, and then to maintain that position. Put negatively, the goal is continuing abstinence with regard to that object, where abstinence is defined precisely as the maintenance of such a position of neutrality.

That is the goal of freedom from root addiction, no less than it is the goal of freedom from any of the derivative addictions. That means that "abstinence" is also the goal of recovery from addiction to attributions.

Freedom from Attribution

Attributions, however, are like food: We can't do without them. They are also like sex: No one *wants* to do without them. Accordingly, the "no usage" criterion cannot be applied to abstinence from attribution. In what, then, does such abstinence consist?

It consists in refraining from *investing* oneself in one's attributions, whatever they may concern. Put positively, it consists in maintaining *neutrality* towards all one's attributions, regardless of their content.

We cannot stop ourselves from making attributions. We do it incessantly. Furthermore, if we made no attributions we would have no science or technology, no art or religion. In fact, without attributions we would not even be able to accomplish daily tasks of the simplest sorts. From infancy, a large part of individual human mental development is the process whereby we first learn to make attributions (to connect things together), and then go on to learn more and more sophisticated strings of attributions. A large part of societal progress also occurs in much the same way. Thus, it would be suicidal to attempt simply to stop making attributions, even if we could.

We can't. All that anyone needs to do to become convinced that we can't is to try. Even to be able to keep our minds free of attributions for a moment or two is an incredibly difficult task. Devotees of any of the many forms of meditation—from Zen breath counting, to the Hindu use of mantras, to contemporary Christian "Centering Prayer"—may literally practice meditation for years before they can detect any significant diminution of mental attributive activity. Nor does it ever cease altogether, except for relatively brief periods followed by a return to everyday consciousness with all its attributions.

So we cannot stop making attributions, even if we wanted to, which we don't. Fortunately, however, we don't have to. In order to free ourselves from addiction to attributions we do not have to give them up altogether, any more than the food addict needs to give up eating or the sex addict needs to give up sex. Rather, we must learn to *relate* to our attributions *differently*, just as the food addict must learn to relate to food differently, the sex addict to sex differently.

We must learn, in effect, not to *care* about our attributions. We must learn a healthy, *positive indifference* toward them, just as the alcoholic must learn such indifference toward alcohol. Once we learn such indifference, we can just let our minds go right on attributing in even the wildest ways, since our attributions will have lost their power over us. We will be free in relationship to them, taking them or leaving them alone as the situation requires of us. We will be just like the recovered food addict who is free in relationship to food, having learned how to eat naturally, taking food when hungry and leaving it alone otherwise.

Shunryu Suzuki was a Japanese Zen master teacher (or "Roshi") who came to the United States in the late 1950s and stayed to found the Zen Center in San Francisco. In *Zen Mind, Beginner's Mind*, which has become a classic, he tells a parable of how to deal with a sheep or cow. What he says applies especially to *unruly* sheep or cattle, we might add. "To give your sheep or cow a large, spacious meadow," writes Suzuki, "is the way to control him."[9]

There is nothing new in what Suzuki says. In fact, it is an ancient insight. The same insight is repeated throughout history, in one spiritual tradition after another, with one formulation or another.

So, for example, we can take the case of Taoism, an ancient, indigenous Chinese religion. The central Taoist idea for escaping universal human bondage is to practice the "way" (the meaning of the term *tao*) of what is called *wu-wei*. That means "nonaction" or "not-doing." However, Taoist nonaction is not to be confused with simple Western *in*action. Indeed, it is perfectly compatible with a high degree of "action" in the ordinary Western sense. It is not a matter of passivity or quiescence. Rather, it is a matter of not *investing* oneself in one's action, and through that investment giving one's very own action power over oneself.

The same basic idea is familiar, as we have already seen with Suzuki, from Zen Buddhism. In its encounter with Buddhism (brought into China from India), Taoism helped to form Zen; in the latter, too, the practice of "nonaction" is central. If anything, in Buddhism in general, whether Zen or not, the enslaving role of what we are here calling "attributions" receives even greater emphasis than it does in Taoism. According to basic Buddhist doctrine, the three ultimate sources of univeral bondage are desire (or attraction), hatred (or aversion), and ignorance. It is nothing but the interplay of those three that gives rise, in fact, to the whole of what is called *Samsara*, the ever spinning wheel of worldly or phenomenal being. Ultimately, Samsara is nothing but a gigantic illusion created by that interplay—an illusion in which we find ourselves trapped without any apparent way out. If we are ever to escape, we must first come to an experience of "enlightenment" in which we see through the illusion. Then we must practice a rigorous discipline of moment-by-moment "mindfulness" in which we *detach* from the continuous stream of our experience—that is, in which, once again, we deliberately hold back from *investing* ourselves in that experience, thereby feeding our desire, hatred, and ignorance. Only in that way can we ever attain liberation.

From Hinduism, the *Bhagavat Gita* tells the story of the warrior Arjuna and the god Krishna, who has incarnated as Arjuna's charioteer and servant. Pausing before the beginning of a monumental battle between opposing forces of the same divided family, Arjuna repents of his own profession as a warrior and is struck by a disabling lethargy. In a poetic dialogue Krishna eventually convinces Arjuna that he must go ahead and join the battle, in accordance with his duty as a warrior. He must even be willing to kill and wound beloved members of his own extended family, since that is what the moment requires of him in his station in life. But he must do so with complete detachment, if he is to avoid acquiring any negative *karma* (inevitable moral consequences, to the agent himself or herself, of any kind of action: a debt that must eventually be paid, if not in this life, then in some subsequent incarnation). He must act as though he were not acting—that is (once again), act without *investing* himself in his actions through his own attributions. In that way, his actions will attain a purity of motivation, or, more precisely, a purity *from* motivation. That is, they will be free of the self-centeredness that otherwise sneaks into even the most apparently altruistic actions, introducing a foreign particle into the underlying intent of the action as altruistic, a particle that adulterates the whole no less surely than a little bit of vinegar will sour a cup of milk. Only Krishna's way of completely disinterested action escapes such adulteration—and with it, the *karma* that would otherwise inevitably accrue.

Especially in the Sufi tradition, Islam contains similar ideas, as does Christianity. Above all in Christian monasticism and mysticism, the necessity of practicing detachment, expressed in whatever terms, is often emphasized.

We have already heard the story of St. Anthony, the great hermit, who had to begin his spiritual pilgrimage by ceasing to cling even to his perfectly natural desire to safeguard his sister's future. As codified by St. Basil the Great in his rules for monastic life, by which Eastern Orthodox monasticism is still governed, and by St. Benedict for Western Christianity, the monastic life has been carefully organized constantly to impel monks in the same direction of divesting themselves of their attachments. Whether living in community or in solitude, monks throughout the centuries have striven toward that same goal. From Evagrius of Pontus, a younger contemporary of St. Anthony who had a lasting influence on both Latin and Orthodox Christian monastic thought and who borrowed from the Greek Stoics the idea of *apatheia* or freedom from the passions, to Thomas Merton in this century, Christian monks have called for such detachment as the way to spiritual perfection. From Origen to Meister Eckhart, from St. Teresa of Avila to St. Therese of Lisieux, from the anonymous author of the fourteenth-century *Cloud of Unknowing* to Edith Stein in the twentieth, Christian mystics, whether monks or not, have done the same.

Inviting Our Impulses Home to Dinner

At a more mundane level, parents must learn the same lesson in trying to raise their children: As with Suzuki's cow, the best way to control an unruly child is to leave it alone. However, parents must leave their children alone *in the right way*. They must leave them alone *lovingly*. That is, they must continue to demonstrate to the child that they love it and will not cease to care for its needs, that they will not abandon it or cut it off from the family in punishment. They must continue to demonstrate such active love in the very process of leaving the child alone. If they can succeed in doing such a thing, then they will *empower* the child to learn *self*-control. From that point on the problem of the unruly child has been removed. Not only has it been removed for the parents (for whom, in fact, there is no longer any "problem" once they lovingly leave the child alone in the first place); it has also been removed for the child.

In Al-Anon, the Twelve Step group for families and friends of alcoholics, the same idea is expressed in the phrase "detachment with love." That is what Al-Anon members are encouraged to practice toward the alcoholics in their lives. That is, they are encouraged to stop "enabling" their alcoholics, but not to stop loving them.

Suzuki's unruly cow is the human mind itself. What he is telling us is that we need to practice loving detachment toward our own mind, that mind which is forever making attributions. We are to give up trying to control our mind, just as the Al-Anon member is to give up trying to control the alcoholic.

Indeed, the more we try to control our own attributions, the less manageable we find them becoming. It is the same for the codependent of an alcoholic. The more the codependent tries to control the drinking behavior of the alcoholic, the more devious and deviant becomes that behavior.

That is even more so for alcoholics themselves. Typically, the harder an alcoholic tries to control his or her drinking, the worse the drinking problem becomes. That process continues until finally the alcoholic "hits bottom" and—gives up. That is, the downward spiral into alcohol addiction continues until the alcoholic is finally ready to surrender the effort to "control" his or her drinking, and is ready, instead, to learn detachment toward alcohol. (In this case, however, there is no special need to be "loving" in the detachment: only an active alcohol addict really "loves alcohol" in the first place).

To recover from addiction to attributions we must also hit bottom. We must come to a point at which we are finally ready to throw in the towel (or perhaps we should say cut the rope) on our endeavor to control the unruly cow. At that point, we are finally ready to learn detachment from attribution.

Because detachment involves hitting such a bottom at which we give up the endeavor to control, to detach from our own attributions is not to fight or oppose them; but it is also not to approve or affirm them. To give up or to surrender is not the same as to give in or to collaborate. "Giving in" to an addiction is the road to total, hopeless enslavement, not part of the road to freedom. Detaching from attributions is not at all giving in to them. Instead, it is simply a matter of not *entertaining* one's attributions—as though they were dinner guests. It is a matter of refraining from *communing* with them,[10] from *investing ourselves in them.*

No matter how long recovering alcoholics may have been abstinent, even if it is a span of many years, from time to time the thought of taking a drink may pop into their minds. That can be occasioned by any number of things. An example could be seeing a television commercial or a highway billboard promoting beer, an advertisement in which sexually attractive persons are shown drinking beer. Such advertisements are designed to invoke a chain of attributions in the viewer (for instance, that the people drinking beer in the advertisement are all sexually attractive, so sexually attractive people drink beer, so drinking beer has something to do with being sexually attractive, so drinking beer will make one sexually attractive oneself, so one should drink some right away). The last link in that chain is the impulse to drink beer (preferably, from the advertiser's point of view, the brand advertised). An abstinent alcoholic is no less susceptible to impulses triggered by such means than anyone else. Despite even long-term abstinence, the possibility of manipulating such an underlying mental mechanism still remains. Most of the time, it is completely beyond our control to stop the process, at least to the stage we have traced it so far. We cannot stop such impulses bombarding us when situational events trigger them. We cannot stop ourselves from feeling them. We have no choice in the process to that point.

However, once the impulse is felt, things change. From that point on, there *is* something that we can do about it. At that point, we do have a choice.

One choice we can make is actively to *entertain* the impulse. To stick with our example, once the impulse to take a drink has been felt the abstinent alcoholic can begin thinking about how good a drink would taste. He or she can go over all the positive memories associated with past drinking, at the same time paying no attention to any negative memories. The alcoholic can work up a good dose of self-pity, if he or she wants to do so—self-pity about not being able to drink like other people. By such means, the alcoholic chooses to *commune* with the idea of taking a drink. The alcoholic rolls that idea around in his or her mind and savors it, just as one might roll a good wine around in one's mouth to the same effect. It is the difference between just *having* a thought (some idea that pops into one's mind uninvited), and actively *thinking* it.

Another choice we have, once we have felt an impulse (any impulse, whether to drink, to flee, to scream, or whatever), is to try to fight it. But for a recovering alcoholic to remain at the level of fighting off recurrent impulses to drink means not yet to have attained freedom from addiction to alcohol, as we have already discussed. Sooner or later, vigilance drops, the will grows weak, or memory dims; and the alcoholic will yield to such recurrent impulses and drink again. For that matter, an observation regularly confirmed by everyday experience is that the more one actively resists a temptation, the stronger it tends to grow. That is because the very effort one must make to resist it requires that one keep it constantly in mind, which tends to reinforce the very attributions that underlie the temptation in the first place.[11]

That leaves us with only one option, our third choice. When we feel an impulse we can choose neither to entertain it nor to resist it, but simply to observe it neutrally, letting it come and go in its own time. That is the option of detachment.

When salespeople come to our doors, to get rid of them we neither have to buy the product they are selling nor resort to rudeness. We can simply hear them out while they make their initial presentation, listening with polite indifference, and then tell them we are not interested and close the door. In the same way, when a thought pops into our minds, we do not have to think it actively for ourselves, nor do we have to try to think it away. Instead, we can simply notice it, observe it with disinterest, and wait for it to leave again.

The thought *will* leave again, sooner or later. It may also very well return again, more or less often, just as salespeople may keep trying the same door. For the newly abstinent alcoholic, the thought of a drink may recur with a frequency that can easily become disheartening, if the alcoholic lets it. But that thought tends to make fewer and fewer return visits, with longer periods in between, as the days of going without a drink mount up. It is just as the most persistent salesperson will sooner or later knock at someone else's door, if met with consistent indifference at ours.

Eventually, the thought of a drink will rarely occur, though sometimes periods of personal crisis and change will bring a greater incidence of occurrences again for a while. When the thought does occur, however, it will now have become habitual for the alcoholic to recoil from it, just as *Alcoholics Anonymous* says. One will have reached the point of neutrality.

The Nonaddictive Mind

In the thirteenth century, Meister Eckhart, founder of German mysticism, praised detachment (German, *Abgeschiedenheit*) as the highest of all possible virtues, greater even than humility or love.[12] According to him, detachment allows us to be completely indifferent even to whether we are in good health or ill. In detachment, it is all one to us; we experience both as pure gifts sent to us by God. The mind that dwells in such perfect detachment is therefore *free* in relationship to both pleasure and pain. Because the detached mind is indifferent to the very distinction between them, it is no longer driven by the pursuit of one and the avoidance of the other.

The detached mind is not free *from* pain, of course. That is, pain will still come from time to time, just as the thought of a drink will sometimes pass the mind of even a long-abstinent alcoholic. But the detached mind is free *in the face of* that pain, when it does come.

Almost seven hundred years later, the twentieth-century philosopher Martin Heidegger, inspired by Eckhart[13] and borrowing another of the latter's terms, recommended "releasement" (German, *Gelassenheit*) toward the many gadgets and devices with which modern technology pervasively surrounds us.[14] According to Heidegger, such releasement permits us to use the products of modern technology with genuine freedom. In releasement toward such things, we are no longer preoccupied with trying to dominate them (an impossible task, by Heidegger's understanding of the nature of modern technology). But neither are we at their mercy: We are able to make use of them, without them coming to use us in turn. When they are there, we are free to use them or not to use them as the concrete situation and our involvement with it make desirable; but we can also get along quite well without them, should that prove necessary or desirable. In short, we are no longer dependent on them.

Alcoholics who have recovered from "a hopeless state of mind and body"[15] have Eckhartian detachment from alcohol. As we have already seen, they have attained a position of neutrality towards it, a calm indifference. Just as, according to Eckhart, pleasure and pain no longer have the power to move a person who has become detached towards both, so has the idea of a drink lost the power to move an alcoholic in that position.

Similarly, recovered sex addicts are in a condition of Heideggerian releasement toward sex. They are able to take it, or leave it alone, as they perceive to be appropriate to their concrete circumstances at the time. No longer obsessed either with having sex or with avoiding it, they are now free in relationship to it.

To be freed from *an* addiction is to be brought into detachment toward the object of the addiction, to be released, in Heidegger's sense, toward it. To be free of addiction *as such* is to practice such detachment and such releasement toward the underlying attributions that constitute root addiction and the root of all other addictions. It is to enter into a general state of detachment, such as

Eckhart and a long string of mystics before and after him, from both Christian and non-Christian traditions, have experienced.

The nonaddictive mind is a detached mind.[16]

"Abandon yourself to God as you understand God. Admit your faults to Him and to your fellows. Clear away the wreckage of your past. Give freely of what you find and join us."[17] That is the way in which the "basic text" (the first 164 pages) in *Alcoholics Anonymous* is summed up on its final page. In the eighteenth century, Jean Pierre de Caussade, a Jesuit priest and noted spiritual director, used the same term—abandonment—to characterize the way of spiritual growth into perfection.[18] What both sources mean by speaking of "abandoning" oneself is the same thing Eckhart calls detachment, Heidegger releasement. It is the condition in which one becomes indifferent toward one's own will, the point at which one occupies a position of neutrality toward *oneself*. It is there, and only there, that one finally attains total freedom from addiction.

The nonaddictive mind is an abandoned mind.

Because it is detached and abandoned, the nonaddictive mind is freed from the sort of circular reasoning that we saw in Chapter 2 to be characteristic of *addictive* mind. By breaking all investment in the attributions that lock one into such circularity of thought— for example, Saint-Exupéry's tippler's attributions of shame to himself for drinking and of the power to alleviate the pain of that shame to the very same activity of drinking—detachment or abandonment breaks out of the circle. It springs the circle open. As opposed to addictive thinking, which is caught in a circle, nonaddictive thinking is thinking that occurs only after thought has wound itself so tight that the whole mechanism finally gets sprung, just like an overwound watch. Thus, whereas the addictive mind is circular, the nonaddictive mind, we might say, is *sprung*.

The nonaddictive mind is no longer wound up tight upon itself, but has been sprung loose. Accordingly, it is no longer beset by the selectivities of perception which we also saw to be characteristic of the addictive mind, in Chapter 2. Because the nonaddictive mind is detached toward itself, there is no longer any chance for underlying motives to form and to distort perception in such ways. Having abandoned all insistence on its own will (on having its own way, even when its own perceptions say it can't), the nonaddictive mind is free to see things as they really present themselves, rather than as it wishes they were. As opposed to being selective in its perceptions, a completely nonaddictive mind is radically *open*.

It is also humble. To be humble does not mean to be cringing and obsequious, nor does it mean to think poorly of oneself. It means, rather, to be truly *aware* of oneself, with all one's strengths and weaknesses, neither exaggerating the first nor minimizing the second. It means to be grateful for what one has, without demanding anything more, or even that one be allowed to keep what has already been given. It means, also, to suffer patiently, with detached, abandoned self-composure, when what one has is taken from one, even when the pain becomes intense. Because the nonaddictive mind is detached toward itself, it no longer feels the need to keep everything focused on itself, constantly worrying about how it appears to others, or even in its own eyes. It is sprung out of the circle of such self-centeredness and into openness toward what is beyond. As an adage that makes the rounds of Twelve Step meetings from time to time sums it up, "Humility is not thinking less of yourself; it's thinking of yourself less."

Thus, as detached, released, and abandoned, the nonaddictive mind is sprung, open, and humble. Only such a mind is truly free of addiction. To strive to develop such a mind oneself, and to help others to develop it, is ultimately the only response adequate to addiction.

·11·

Addiction and Responsibility

Reacting and Responding

To *react* to something that happens is to empower that to which one is reacting. To *respond* to something that happens is to empower oneself.

I have had a long day at work. My classes have not gone well, and I have had some unpleasant encounters with a few of my students who came to my office to complain about their grades on a recent test. I am behind in my class preparation as well as in my administrative work for my department. A committee meeting at the end of the day has caused me to be late leaving the office. To top it all off, traffic is unusually heavy and it takes me an extra half hour to get home. When I finally do walk in the door to my house, my wife immediately begins complaining that we were supposed to go to a parent-teacher conference before dinner, but she was forced to go alone when I did not arrive home on time. I grow angry and raise my voice to my wife, complaining in my own turn about her insensitivity to how tired and overworked I am. Slamming down my briefcase on the kitchen table, I retreat in a huff to my study, where I intend to pout until my wife comes in and apologizes. When she doesn't, I just grow more irritated.

In that example, all I am doing is *reacting* to situations as they develop. I am letting events "push my buttons and pull my strings," and I am dancing to whatever tune they select. They are in control of me, not I of them—or of myself!

Some of those events are external (for example, my wife's complaining). Those outside events first trigger attributions in me (her complaining is a sign of her insensitivity to my needs). Those attributions, in turn, trigger emotional reactions in me (irritation and anger). That is the first cycle of reaction.

The attributions that form in me in reaction to outside events are themselves internal events, as are the emotions that form in reaction to the attributions. As the external events first triggered these internal ones, the latter now in turn trigger externally expressed actions or behaviors on my part (in the example, my anger causes me to slam down my briefcase and storm off to my study). That is the second cycle of reaction.

The process continues on and on from there. My actions themselves trigger attributions in others (for instance, my wife may attribute my storming off as just one more sign of the low priority she thinks I give to her and the rest of my family). Those attributions trigger emotions in them (my wife's already present irritation toward me grows stronger). Those emotions trigger actions on their part (my wife throws my dinner down the garbage disposal and tosses my briefcase in the trash can), which trigger more attributions that trigger more emotions in me (when I finally come out of my study and see what she has done, my anger builds toward rage), which trigger further actions on my part (I go out and get drunk), and so forth, round and round and round again.

It is as circular as the thinking of an addict, and just as enslaving. When I am reacting in such ways, I may feel quite in control of myself, and I may think that I am exercising free and sovereign power over my own choices and actions at every step of the way. That is precisely how addicts often feel, even when they are in the most advanced stages of their addictions. In both cases, however, the freedom is purely illusory. There is really no freedom there at all. Insofar as we remain at the level of reaction, events are in control, and we are at their mercy.

In contrast, to *respond* to an event is to reclaim our own choices and actions. It is to reassert our right and capacity to *self*-control in the fullest sense. That is a sense having nothing to do with moralistic rigidity (the incapacity to break a prohibition that we have heard Erikson mention), but in which one attains the freedom of genuine self-expression. To respond, rather than to react, to an event is to issue a *rejoinder* to the event, as it were—a rejoinder in which I give voice to my own uniqueness in answer to the uniqueness of the initial event, as it concretely displays itself to me in my experience of it.

We have all experienced such moments. They are those moments in which we suddenly find ourselves completely *open and receptive* to everything that is going on around us, down to its finest nuances and details. Sometimes such a moment comes when we are at work, wholly absorbed in doing a task for which our talents and training have prepared us perfectly, where we no longer need to check ourselves against any set of directions (mental or otherwise) or await the judgment of any external authority (or even any internalized one) to be assured of the quality of our work. At other times, we find ourselves entering such a state of awareness when we are at play.

There are moments in playing tennis or some other sport involving competition with another player when one ceases to have to struggle to anticipate the movements of the opponent and position oneself for a reply. Instead, one seems able effortlessly to know exactly what is going to occur from one shot to the next. One just as effortlessly meets whatever the opponent casts one's way, and meets it with just the right countering, rejoining return shot.

Similar moments occur in solitary sports, for example, in noncompetitive skiing or bicycling. While we are engaging in one or the other of those two sports, there come moments when one feels wholly in tune with the slope and the skis, or with the bicycle and the road—and with oneself.

For some of us, such moments come while we are dancing. They are those moments when we and our partner seem to become one with the music. Each note calls out to us, and calls out from us in response just the right motion. It is a motion wholly appropriate to the music that invites it, yet at the same time wholly free. It is a uniquely nuanced motion, one stamped indelibly with an identifying mark expressing the individuality of the dancing couple that sets it apart from all the equally wholly appropriate, wholly unique responses to the same note that might be made by all the other dancing couples on the same dance floor.

Genuinely and fully *responding* to a situation, as opposed to merely *reacting* to it, requires, first of all, that we be fully *open* to that situation. That is, it requires that we approach it without prejudice and prejudgment, demanding of it that it give us what we want of it. We must be free in relationship to all the expectancies we have towards the situation, expectancies that come from our investing ourselves in all the attributions that inevitably form in our minds as changes occur in the situation from moment to moment. Insofar as we invest ourselves in those attributions, we block ourselves from the possibility of encountering our situation as it actually addresses us. As a consequence, we block ourselves from any possibility of responding to it by making a rejoinder, in our own behavior, to the unique requirements of each and every unfolding moment. Only if we let ourselves see what needs to be done, do we have the option of doing it.

If we are not open to the situation as it actually is, there is no way that our actions in that situation will succeed. They will not be able to avoid going astray. Distorted by our selectivities of perception, our actions will miss the mark. We will "sin," in that original and still fundamental sense. That is not a matter of our actions failing to conform to some external standard of conduct. It is a matter, rather, of our actions becoming distorted at the level of their own nature—the level of their own definitive intentions, so that while we aim at accomplishing one thing we actually end up accomplishing the opposite (as in St. Paul's anguished cry, with which we closed Chapter 6). Our own actions themselves are thereby dis-owned.

In reaction to the way in which our actions themselves are so disowned (robbed of the very intention that originally defines them), we ourselves disown them, as Pilate disowned responsibility for the crucifixion of Jesus. After all, what they accomplished is not what we intended. So we no longer see ourselves in them. We can, therefore, wash our hands of them, all in "good conscience."

However, the cost of such an unblemished conscience is no less than relinquishing our claim to being efficacious agents. We keep our consciences pure in such a way only by robbing ourselves of our own actions, giving up rights to them and turning them over to external events. Our actions cease truly to be actions at all, and instead become mere *reactions*. We keep our good reputations, at least in our own eyes, only by losing our very selves.

Addiction as an Incapacitation for Response

Addiction deprives addicts of the capacity to respond.

Far too often, the only question asked about addiction and responsibility is the question of who is responsible "for" addiction— that is, who is to *blame* for it. Are addicts to blame for their own addictions, or are they victims of powers beyond their control? That is the sort of question that is typically raised, if any consideration at all is given to the connection between addiction, on the one hand, and responsibility, on the other.

"Who's responsible for this?" asks the teacher angrily when she walks into class and sees expletives written all over the blackboard. That is, she wants to know who did it.

Who's responsible for this person becoming addicted to heroin? When we ask that, what we want to know is who did it. Who addicted this person to heroin? Who got him or her hooked on it? Whom are we to blame?

Most of the time, the answer to that question is, "Nobody." No one at all is to blame for most addicts becoming addicted. There are some cases in which some villain really is involved. Some evil pusher, perhaps, gets kicks out of waylaying unwary passersby and addicting them to heroin, cocaine, nicotine, or whatever. Maybe it is not even that bad. Maybe it is not just for the thrill of it, but because the pusher has a habit of his or her own to maintain, and pushing is the only or the easiest way to raise the money to support that habit.

At any rate, except insofar as a sort of "pushing" is simply built into the institutional framework of modern life itself, most addicts don't get pushed into addiction. Rather, as William S. Burroughs wrote, they just drift into it for lack of any strong motivation in any other direction.

Unfortunately, however, there *is* a kind of pushing of potential objects of addiction built right into modern life. It is built in by way of advertisements, peer pressure, folklore, family example, novels, movies, TV, and so on. It belongs to the very nature of a modern consumer society. After all, it goes with a consumer-oriented economy to foster consumption, and addicts really help keep up the demand for a product.

Finally that is not reducible to any cynical direct manipulation, any orchestrated, intentional endeavor to push drugs or other potential objects of addiction on naive consumers. Rather, reaching far beyond any such intentional manipulation, there are essential addiction-fostering mechanisms built into the very fabric of consumer society as such, especially into the very nature of advertising.

"The importance of advertising," as social critic Christopher Lasch has written," . . . does not lie in its manipulation of the consumer or the direct influence on consumer choices." Rather, Lasch continues, "The point is that it makes the consumer an addict unable to live without increasingly sizeable doses of externally provided stimulation." A few sentences later he concludes, "Ideologies, no matter how appealing and powerful, cannot shape the structure of perception and conduct unless they are embedded in daily experiences that appear to confirm them. In our society, those experiences teach people to want a never-ending supply of new toys and drugs."[1]

The same pervasive materialism of modern consumer society also blocks common access to sources of genuine spirituality. As a consequence, for the mass of people there is nothing to provide the sort of strong motivation away from addiction that we have heard both William S. Burroughs and Carl Jung mention. By distorting spiritual longing in a materialistic direction that cannot ultimately bring satisfaction, modern society again strengthens the tendency toward addiction as an apparent alternative.

Insofar as the fostering of addiction occurs in such indirect but pervasive ways in our society, to try to isolate individuals or groups whom we can blame for addiction is nothing but a way of passing the buck. It is a natural and understandable reaction to the frightening incidence of addiction in our society; but that is all it is—a reaction. It misses the mark, precisely because it fails even to see the real problem, which is the extent to which fostering addiction is built into the very fabric of modern Western society. Looking for someone to blame is part of the problem, not part of the solution.

That applies not only to the attempt to blame "pushers," whether individual or corporate. It also applies to the attempt to blame addicts themselves. That is not because addicts do not contribute to their own addictions through their own choices and actions. As we have argued throughout this book, the choices we make and the actions we perform play a crucial role in whether we become addicts or not. We do not become addicts *despite* ourselves, as we have insisted repeatedly.

Following Burroughs, we have been no less insistent that (with at most rare exceptions) no one sets out to become an addict, either. That is, addiction is rarely if ever the result of any clear and deliberate decision to become an addict, as one might decide to become a lawyer or a social activist.

To that extent, addicts become addicted through ignorance, rather than through intention. In accordance with a principle generally acknowledged at least since Aristotle, one can reasonably be held accountable for actions performed out of ignorance only if the ignorance itself was one's own fault—only if one truly "should have known better," given readily available information, no disturbance of one's faculties, and so forth.

To restate Lasch's observation in other terms, consumer society as such (and not just by way of blameworthy individuals or groups within that society) fosters addiction because it encourages a purely *reactive* way of living. In such a way of living, one is deprived of any meaningful opportunity to exercise control over oneself or what happens to one. But as we have seen (in Chapter 8), the ultimate appeal of addiction is that it permits addicts to *feel* precisely that— "in control." The truth of the matter, which is that addiction is actually the most extreme form of bondage to a purely reactive mode of existence, is not something of which addicts become genuinely aware (in the sense that de Mello, for example, gives that term) until they have sunk all the way down into addiction and "hit bottom."

It is as a culmination of the general process of dis-ownment already inherent in modern society as such that addiction robs addicts of the capacity to respond to events, rather than merely to react to them. The temptation towards addiction lies in unconscious rebellion against a purely reactive life as spiritually deadening. Addiction is a form of rebellion against the bondage of reactive living by endeavoring to reassert "control" over oneself and one's life. But under the illusion it creates that practicing the addiction grants one such control, addiction actually enslaves one all the more hopelessly to pure reaction. Addictions robs addicts of even their rebellion against reactive living; it transforms that very rebellion into new links in the reactive chain.

By thus enchaining us in reaction, addiction makes us no longer even *able* to respond. In that sense, it is literally a contradiction to say that addicts themselves are "responsible" for their own addictions: As addicts, they are no longer even response-able.

Becoming Response-Able and Assuming One's Responsibilities

Only someone who is able to respond is in any position to assume his or her "responsibilities." Accordingly, if the goal of rehabilitation for addicts is to make them once again (or for the first time) "responsible" members of society—men and women, that is, who fulfill their various responsibilities—the only place to begin is by helping them to regain their capacity to respond.

Paradoxically, the only way to restore addicts' response-ability is by giving them responsibilities. That is, we must substitute care*giving* to addicts for care*taking* from them.

To that extent, it is no different from bringing up a child. Effective parenting requires that we give greater and greater responsibilities to our children as they grow. By giving them responsibilities appropriate to their growing capacities, we allow them to develop skills of their own, and the self-esteem that goes with them. At the same time, by letting them do for themselves whatever they prove able to do, we concretely demonstrate to them our respect and trust for them, showing our confidence in them. In turn, our confidence in them increases their own confidence in themselves, empowering them to reach out even further, toward greater and greater responsibilities. Eventually, as our caregiving continues in reciprocal response with their risk taking, our children become mature adults in their own right. Then we are faced with our culminating task as parents: The task of completely letting our children go, to live out their own lives independently of us—the task of giving them over entirely to their own care.

In the same way, if we would help addicts grow in recovery from addiction, we must be careful to give them as much responsibility as they can reasonably handle. At least for addicts who are biologically adult and, apart from their addictions, have no mental or physical limitations so severe as to require that an exception be made, that means that we must give addicts *complete responsibility for themselves.*

Lest that be misunderstood, we should recall a remark from Chapter 6, that it is not "enabling" to do such things as take to the hospital an alcoholic who, while drinking, has received an injury requiring immediate medical attention. To give addicts complete responsibility for themselves does not mean to turn our back on them when they are in need, any more than letting our children leave us and enter into their own adult lives means refusing ever again to help them when they run into troubles. Giving either addicts or our own grown children responsibility for their own lives is not the same thing as deserting them.

For example, if one of our adult children comes into financial difficulties, there is nothing in principle wrong with us either lending or giving him or her monetary assistance. What is wrong— because it is debilitating for the recipient of the gesture—is to do that in a way that enables the adult child to act as if an adult child is no more than a child, rather than also an adult. That is, what is debilitating is to give assistance in a way that robs adult children of responsibility for their own lives by fostering continuing dependence, financial or otherwise, on their parents.

It is not only in giving financial assistance that we must be careful not to shift over from caregiving toward our adult children into caretaking from them. It is also in giving any other form of assistance. Sometimes, our adult children may be well off financially, but in need of emotional support. We may want to offer them our approval, advice, or admonition. Those, too, can be given in ways that are debilitating to the recipients, or in ways that are empowering of them.

A grown daughter comes to her father, very upset. Her husband has asked for a divorce. The father hugs his daughter. Then he tells her she is always welcome to come live with him again. He goes on to remind her that his opinion of her husband was never good, and that he had warned her about him before they were ever married. He wishes she had listened to him then, he says. That would have saved her all the heartache now. At any rate, the father concludes, it is time for her to come back to her real home and to forget all about her erstwhile husband.

Or imagine a grown son coming to his mother for help with managing his monthly bills. No sooner do they sit down at the table together to begin going through his financial records, than the mother takes over. She begins doing all the arranging, recording, and calculating for her son, meanwhile telling him she would be willing to handle his checkbook for him so he wouldn't have to worry about it. Why not just turn his paychecks over to her, along with his checkbook? Then he could give her his bills as they arrived in the mail, and she could write out his checks for him to sign. When the bills were all paid, she could then let him know how much he had left over for spending money.

In those two examples, emotional support is given in a destructive way. As actually delivered, it does not really offer support at all. Instead, it offers a chance to be "taken care of." The father's words chip away at the daughter's self-esteem; the mother's chip away at the son's. Both father and mother discourage their children from trying to take care of themselves, and invite them to continue to let their parents take care of them instead. They reduce them to the status of the childish children they used to be, the ones their parents would (unconsciously, we can charitably assume) have them always remain.

There is nothing empowering about such an enabling "gift." It is debilitating. It fosters in the recipient a condition of general dependency.

A condition of general dependency is one in which we are no longer able to respond to events, but can only react to them. That, as we have just been discussing, is precisely a condition ripe for addiction.

To offer assistance to any adult in such a way is, therefore, indirectly to foster addiction. All the more so, to offer such distorted assistance to addicts is to foster addiction, under the very guise of combating it. Solely by the mode of delivery, even aside from all conscious intention, such "assistance" actually encourages addicts to remain in a general condition of dependency—the very condition that directly encourages addicts to remain in their addictions.

In contrast, if we are truly to help addicts overcome their addiction, we must help them to assume responsibility for themselves, rather than encourage them to remain in a condition of dependency in which others take responsibility for them. We do that, not by blaming addicts for their addictions, but by challenging them with the possibility of recovery. Every time a codependent practices "detachment with love," just such a challenge is offered. The same challenge is issued every time an employer sits down with an alcoholic employee and calmly discusses the latter's drinking problem, offering clear alternatives between which the employee must choose (for example, the choice between entry into an addiction-recovery program or receiving notice of termination of employment the next time drinking interferes with his or her work). Whenever addicts are directly, lovingly confronted with the consequences of their addictions, they are challenged in that empowering, caregiving way.

To return to our two examples of the father with his daughter and the mother with her son, things might have been handled differently in any number of ways, to empower the two adult children rather than to disable them. We make only a few suggestions for each alternative situation.

The father might have begun just as in the example, by hugging his daughter and assuring her that she was always welcome at his home. But then, instead of giving her an open-ended invitation to return home to live with him, he might have asked her what *she* was thinking of doing. If she had no idea, he might well have suggested that she come back home for the time being, but then promised to help her find a place of her own as soon as possible. The specific response (like every true response, as opposed to mere reactions) would depend upon the specific circumstances. At any rate, whatever the circumstances, the father would have invited his daughter to talk about her own perceptions of the situation and the options it afforded her. He would have encouraged her to explore those options in her own thinking, as well as in discussion with him. He would have encouraged her to talk to others besides himself—mother, siblings, friends, other confidants, whoever might be able to help. Through it all, he would have simply *listened* in an active way, helping her to accept her own emotional turmoil by showing her, through that simple, attentive, detached, nondirective listening, his own acceptance and love of her, his daughter, in and beyond her present difficulties.

The mother whose son approaches her for help in managing his finances would have offered him just that—*help*. That is, she would have let *him* do the actual work, the arranging, calculating, and so forth, with perhaps an occasional suggestion or pointer from her. If he got stuck with something, she might even have taken over some of the paperwork for him, but only to show him how it was done. After giving him an example of how to do it, she would immediately have turned the work back to him, letting him try again. Under certain circumstances, she might even have gone on to suggest that he let her be his financial manager for a while, but certainly not without his participation, so that she could show him what she was doing and explain why. That way, he would learn as soon as possible to dispense with her services and manage his finances for himself.

When children who are old enough to begin learning how to fix the flat tires on their bicycles come to adults for help, the adults will often just fix the tires themselves, rather than showing the children how to do it. After all, it is much easier and quicker for the adults that way.

Such behavior enables the children to keep on riding their bicycles, to be sure; but it does so only at the price of robbing them of an opportunity to develop their own capacities. Like all enabling, as we have seen before, it really *disables*.

It is no accident that many recovering alcoholics in Alcoholics Anonymous and other recovering addicts in other recovery programs testify that one major ingredient in their early recovery was assuming responsibility for small tasks associated with AA or other recovery group meetings. Many alcoholics took a crucial step towards recovery by doing no more than taking responsibility for cleaning up after themselves at the end of a meeting—no more than emptying their own ashtrays and throwing away their own disposable coffee cups when the meeting was over. Such small tasks, willingly undertaken on their own initiative, without anyone yelling at them to do so or admonishing them that they should, are often the first concrete signs that alcoholics and other addicts have begun to regain their ability to respond, their response-ability.

"One of the neat things about self-help groups [such as AA]," writes Thomas W. Perrin, an expert on alcoholism and private counselor for alcoholics and addicts and who is himself an alcoholic in recovery, as well as the adult child of alcoholic parents, "is that they teach responsibility at basic levels, like making coffee, or taking up the collection, or just locking up at night. Responsibility is broken down into manageable pieces, and we're not overwhelmed by our tasks." As Perrin has come to realize, the way to teach responsibility is by freely giving out responsibilities, however small they may be. It is by freely assuming or taking up these small responsibilities that addicts reclaim their ability to respond and grow in it: "And then we find that we gain self-esteem by being reliable and responsible. That is new information! Being irresponsible becomes extinguished in favor of being responsible, because the latter feels so much better than the illusion of freedom provided by the former."[2]

The Response to Addiction

Whether we consider it in terms of the addict or of the codependent, of the individual or of the society, of resisting initial addiction or of recovering from addiction already rampant, there is finally only one response adequate to addiction: The restoration and reclamation of responsibility.

First and above all, that means the restoration and reclamation of response-*ability*—of the very *capacity* to respond. Addiction as such diminishes that capacity, robbing addicts of it in direct proportion to the depths of the addiction. So do what we might call all addictionogenic (addiction engendering) conditions: all acts of enabling, no matter how indirect, as well as all the ways in which individuals and societies directly foster dependencies of any kind, whether through blatantly pushing drugs on children or through subliminally reinforcing a consumer mentality through advertising. Attempting to exercise one's ability to respond by assuming one's responsibilities in a society where such conditions are prevalent is like trying to breathe with a heavy weight on one's chest.

We must give one another air, and room to breathe it. We must grant one another space to exercise our capacities to respond.

What is required is not at all a matter of dreaming up new burdens or obligations to lay upon ourselves or others. We all have all the burdens we can bear, if we only begin to try fully responding to the everyday events that take place in our own situations. What is required is simply to clear the way for such response to occur.

We need to remember that we do not make people more respon-sible by berating them for their irresponsibility. Telling people how irresponsible they are only helps implant images of themselves in their own minds as *incapable* of responsibility. That ultimately fur-thers the very irresponsibility we are trying to combat.

Nor do we make people more responsible by admonishing them to assume their responsibilities. Once again, to admonish people to be responsible really tells them that they are *not* responsible: If they were, they wouldn't have to be admonished all the time.

Instead, to help people become responsible, we need to treat them as response-able. We need to treat them as able to respond, and not treat them as ir-response-able by telling them how irrespon-sible they are or by admonishing them about what we take to be their responsibilities. We have to treat them as we want them more fully to *be*. Only by acknowledging and respecting the ways, how-ever small, in which they are already able to respond, rather than merely to react, do we give others the room they need to exercise that very power to respond. It is only through regular, vigorous exercise that the capacity to respond can grow, just as it is only through regular, vigorous exercise that muscles grow. To make peo-ple more responsible, we must let them use their response-ability.

In turn, our ability to respond is itself grounded in this, that something in our experience presents itself to us as *requiring* a response. To respond to an event is to answer back to it. But we can answer *back* only if we are first of all *addressed*—called upon *to* give answer. What first and last calls out response-ability is being addressed. It is being challenged or invoked, being called out and forth. It is having a question put to us.

The crying of a child puts a question to us. So do the honest tears of someone we have hurt by breaking our promises to be home, promises we forgot once we began drinking, drugging, eat-ing, talking, or in some other way practicing one of our addictions. So does the detached love of the spouses who show the addicts in their lives enough respect to let them clean up their own messes, or the caring honesty of employers offering clear options to addicted employees.

An alcoholic in recovery telling an AA meeting the story of what it used to be like, what happened, and what it is like now, puts a question to the uncertain newcomers huddled in the corners or trying to hide in the back rows. Such a story challenges the new-comers, calling out for response.

The call has the power to awaken the ability to respond in those newcomers. By virtue of its own simple honesty, the story of one alcoholic who has found freedom from alcohol has the power to cut through all the years of addictive reaction and invoke in its hearers the long dormant capacity to answer back—to respond with equal simplicity and honesty. Even if the exact words are never spoken, one ex-drunk's story of recovery, simply recounted, tells those who are still drinking that they never again have to take another drink, not ever, so long as they live, if only they don't want to.

No challenge could be more powerful, not for a group of drunks. It has the power to set them free, for it strips them bare of all their pretenses and leaves it all up to them. The challenge calls those who hear it forth into responsibility because it trusts in, and thereby unleashes, their response-ability. What other response is really possible to someone who truly hears the challenge put by such a story? What other response but once and for all to give up drinking and accept responsibility?

Addiction challenges addicts to accept their own powerlessness, their inability to "control" things. It challenges them to accept the fact that they are not God.[3] It challenges them to acknowledge that they are called upon, not to control, but only to *respond* to what is given us all, rich and poor, good and bad alike: respond to it by singing, dancing, weeping, crying, loving, and, in general, living and dying. The ability to respond springs from that very acknowledgment. It is set free by it.

Responsibility comes naturally to those who grow in their ability to respond. Our addictions call us out into such growth. The response to addiction is to learn to respond.

We have only to listen in order to hear, and then to answer.

Notes

Introduction: The Philosophy of Addiction

1. For example: Herbert Fingarette, *Heavy Drinking: The Myth of Alcoholism as a Disease* (Berkeley: University of California Press, 1988); Stanton Peele, *Diseasing of America: Addiction Treatment Out of Control* (Lexington, Mass.: Lexington Books, 1989); Morris Kokin with Ian Walker, *Women Married to Alcoholics: Help and Hope for Nonalcoholic Partners* (New York: William Morrow, 1989); Stan J. Katz & Aimee Liu, *The Codependency Conspiracy* (New York: Warner, 1991); Stanton Peele & Archie Brodsky, with Mary Arnold, *The Truth About Addiction and Recovery: The Life-Process Program for Outgrowing Destructive Habits* (New York: Simon & Schuster, 1991); Carol Tavris, *The Mismeasure of Woman* (New York: Simon & Schuster, 1992).

2. The only exception that might be worth mentioning is Herbert Fingarette, who has devoted various articles and one entire book (see note 1, *Heavy Drinking*) to alcoholism. However, in those works Fingarette is not writing as a philosopher, but as an expert on alcoholism; his purpose is primarily polemical, as the subtitle to his book indicates.

Chapter 1: The Experience of Addiction

1. William S. Burroughs, *Junky* (New York: Penguin Books, 1953), p. xv.

2. *Alcoholics Anonymous*, 3rd ed. (New York: Alcoholics Anonymous World Services, 1976), pp. xxvi–xxvii.

3. Nelson Algren, *The Man With the Golden Arm* (New York: Random House, 1947), p. 56.

4. *Alcoholics Anonymous*, p. xxvi.

5. Arnold Washton and Donna Boundy, *Willpower's Not Enough* (New York: Harper & Row, 1989), pp. 36–37.

6. I have borrowed the distinction between involving the total person and involving the person totally from Patrick L. Bourgeoise, *The Religious Within*

Experience and Existence: A Phenomenological Investigation (Pittsburgh: Duquesne University Press, 1990).

7. Washton and Boundy, *Willpower's Not Enough.*

Chapter 2: The Addictive Mind

1. Antoine de Saint-Exupéry, *The Little Prince* (San Diego, New York, London: Harcourt Brace Jovanovich, 1971), pp. 50–52.
2. *Rocky Mountain News*, May 16, 1988.
3. *Alcoholics Anonymous*, p. 24.
4. Ibid., p. 36.
5. G. Alan Marlatt and Judith R. Gordon, *Relapse Prevention: Maintenance Strategies in the Treatment of Addictive Behavior* (New York: Guilford Press, 1985), pp. 191–192.
6. *Alcoholics Anonymous*, p. 569.
7. Gerald G. May, *Addiction and Grace* (San Francisco: Harper & Row, 1988), p. 36.
8. Gregory Bateson, "The Cybernetics of 'Self': A Theory of Alcoholism," *Psychiatry*, 34 (February 1971): 8.
9. Ibid., p. 12.
10. *Alcoholics Anonymous*, p. 25.

Chapter 3: Defining Addiction

1. May, *Addiction and Grace.*
2. Mark Keller, "On Defining Alcoholism: With Comment on Some Other Relevant Words," in Lisansky Gomberg, Helene Raskin White, and John A. Carpenter, eds., *Alcohol, Science, and Society Revisited* (Ann Arbor: University of Michigan; and New Brunswick, N.J.: Rutgers Center of Alcohol Studies, 1982), p. 127.
3. Harold Kalant, "The Nature of Addiction: An Analysis of the Problem," in Avram Goldstein, ed., *Molecular and Cellular Aspects of the Drug Addictions* (New York: Springer, 1989), pp. 17, 20.
4. Burroughs, *Junky*, p. xv.
5. Ibid.
6. Ibid., p. 22.
7. Goldstein, *Molecular and Cellular Aspects*, p. xiv.
8. Keller, "On Defining Alcoholism," p. 127.
9. Quoted in Goldstein, *Molecular and Cellular Aspects*, p. xiii.
10. Ibid., p. xii.
11. Burroughs, *Junky*, p. xvi.
12. *Alcoholics Anonymous*, p. 151.

13. Burroughs, *Junky*, p. xv.

14. Ibid., p. xvi.

Chapter 4: Delimiting the Scope of Addiction: "Substance Addiction" and "Process Addiction"

1. *Alcoholics Anonymous*, pp. 37–38.

2. Anne Wilson Schaeff, *Escape from Intimacy* (San Francisco: Harper & Row, 1989).

3. For a review of recent research see Howard Cappell and Janet Greeley, "Alcohol and Tension Reduction: An Update on Research and Theory," in Howard T. Blane and Kenneth E. Leonard, eds., *Psychological Theories of Drinking and Alcoholism* (New York: The Guilford Press, 1987).

4. For a review of recent research see Mark S. Goldman, Sandra A. Brown, and Bruce A. Christiansen, "Expectancy Theory: Thinking About Drinking," in Blane and Leonard, *Psychological Theories of Drinking*.

5. Eli Coleman, psychologist at the University of Minnesota, quoted in "Do People Get Hooked on Sex?" *Time*, June 4, 1990, p. 72.

6. *Diagnostic and Statistical Manual of Mental Disorders, 3rd ed.* (Washington, D.C.: American Psychiatric Association, 1987).

7. See Capell and Greeley, "Alcohol and Tension Reduction."

8. Stanton Peele, *The Meaning of Addiction: Compulsive Experience and Its Interpretation* (Lexington, Mass: Lexington Books, 1985), especially pp. 97–104.

Chapter 5: Classifying Addiction: Disease, Disorder, or Misconduct?

1. *Alcoholics Anonymous*, p. 64.

2. May, *Addiction and Grace*, p. 20.

3. George Vaillant, *The Natural History of Alcoholism* (Cambridge: Harvard University Press, 1983), p. 308.

4. E. M. Jellinek, *The Disease Concept of Alcoholism* (New Haven, Conn., and New Brunswick, N.J.: College and University Press in association with Hillhouse Press, 1960), pp. 11–12.

5. Ibid., p. 12.

6. For instance, throughout the "basic text" of *Alcoholics Anonymous* (the first 164 pages), Wilson often calls alcoholism an "illness," a "sickness," or a "malady," but carefully avoids the term *disease*.

7. For a good suggestion of the multiplicity of factors involved in the test case of alcoholism, see Terrence M. Donovan, "An Etiologic Model of Alcoholism," *The American Journal of Psychiatry*, 143, 1 (January 1986): 1–11.

8. For discussion of the case of alcoholism, see W. Miles Cox, "Personality Theory and Research," in Blane and Leonard, *Psychological Theories of Drinking*.

9. For a survey of the sociological theories pertaining to alcoholism, which can be taken as indicative for addiction in general, see Helene Raskin White,

"Sociological Theories of the Etiology of Alcoholism," in Gomberg, White, and Carpenter, *Alcohol, Science, and Society.*
10. Vaillant, *Natural History of Alcoholism,* p. 17.
11. *Acloholics Anonymous,* p. 30.
12. Vaillant, *Natural History of Alcoholism,* p. 309.
13. *Alcoholics Anonymous,* pp. 32–33.

Chapter 6: The Essence of Addiction

1. Wulstan Mork, *The Benedictine Way* (Petersham, Mass.: St. Bede's Publications, 1987), p. vii.
2. Stanton Peele, with Archie Brodsky, *Love and Addiction* (New York: Taplinger Publishing Co., 1975), p. 17.
3. For a good discussion of the application of social learning theory to alcoholism, see David B. Abrams and Raymond S. Niaura, "Social Learning Theory," in Blane and Leonard, *Psychological Theories of Drinking.*
4. *Alcoholics Anonymous,* p. 188.
5. Ibid., p. 21.
6. Martin Heidegger, *Being and Time,* translated by John Macquarrie and Edward Robinson (New York: Harper & Row, 1962), pp. 158–159 (p. 122 in standardized pagination).
7. Concerning how basic modern social institutions foster addiction, and how institutions or organizations can come to function both as objects of addiction for individuals and as addicts in their own right, see Anne Wilson Schaef, *When Society Becomes an Addict* (San Francisco: Harper & Row, 1987), and Anne Wilson Schaef and Diane Fassel, *The Addictive Organization* (San Francisco: Harper & Row, 1988).
8. Romans 7: 19–24.

Chapter 7: The Meaning of Addiction

1. Wilson's letter to Jung, and Jung's response, can be found in *The Language of the Heart: Bill W.'s Grapevine Writings* (New York: The AA Grapevine, 1988), pp. 276–281.
2. See Bruce K. Alexander, Stanton Peele, Patricia F. Hadaway, Stanley J. Morse, Archie Brodsky, and Barry L. Beyerstein, "Adult, Infant, and Animal Addiction," which is Chapter 5 in Peele's *The Meaning of Addiction.*
3. Matthew 19:16–22.
4. Matthew 6:34.
5. See Aristotle, *Nicomachean Ethics,* Book II, especially Chaps. 8 and 9.
6. May, *Addiction and Grace,* p. viii.
7. A line often heard in AA meetings, based on *Alcoholics Anonymous,* p. 60: "We claim spiritual progress rather than spiritual perfection."

8. *Alcoholics Anonymous*, p. xxvii.

9. William S. Burroughs, *Naked Lunch* (New York: Grove Press, 1959).

Chapter 8: The Root of Addiction

1. Goldstein, *Molecular and Cellular Aspects*, p. xiii.

2. Thomas W. Perrin, *I Am an Adult Who Grew Up in an Alcoholic Family* (New York: Continuum, 1991), especially pp. 74–89.

3. For a summary of the research on alcoholism see W. Miles Cox, "Personality Theory and Research," in Blane and Leonard, *Psychological Theories of Drinking*.

4. With reference to alcoholism, for a discussion of the anthropological and sociological research, respectively, see Dwight B. Heath, "In Other Cultures, They Also Drink," and Helene Raskin White, "Sociological Theories of the Etiology of Alcoholism," in Gomberg, White, and Carpenter, *Alcoholism, Science, and Society*.

5. Peele, *The Meaning of Addiction*, pp. 97–98.

6. Peele with Brodsky, *Love and Addiciton*, p. 52.

7. See Goldman, Brown, and Christiansen, "Expectancy Theory."

8. A nice, brief treatment of the multiplicity of risk factors for alcoholism, which in principle can be extended to addiction in general, is to be found in Donovan, "An Etiologic Model of Alcoholism."

9. J. Keith Miller, *A Hunger for Healing: The Twelve Steps as a Classic Guide for Christian Spiritual Growth* (San Francisco: Harper, 1991), p. 5.

10. Stanley Schachter and Jerome E. Singer, "Cognitive, Social, and Physiological Determinants of Emotional State," *Psychological Review*, 69 (1962).

Chapter 9: "Right Effort" Towards Addiction

1. Erik H. Erikson, *Gandhi's Truth* (New York: W. W. Norton and Co., 1969), p. 145.

2. For a general discussion, see Ivan D. Illich, *Celebration of Awareness* (New York: Doubleday, 1970). In a variety of books Illich has applied his analysis to various specific insitutions—including education, in *Deschooling Society* (New York: Harper & Row, 1970).

3. To date, Anne Wilson Schaef has done the most along these lines (see note 7 to Chapter 6).

4. *RB 1980: The Rule of St. Benedict*, edited by Timothy Fry (Collegeville, Minn.: Liturgical Press, 1981), p. 165 (Prologue 48–49).

5. *Alcoholics Anonymous*, p. 152.

6. Ibid., p. 153.

7. Ibid., p. 164.

Chapter 10: Freedom From Addiction: The Nonaddictive Mind

1. David Berenson, quoted in Barbara Yoder, *The Recovery Resource Book* (New York: Simon & Schuster, 1990), p. 16.

2. *Alcoholics Anonymous*, p. 31.

3. Ibid., p. 135.

4. Perrin, *I Am An Adult*, p. 112.

5. Anthony de Mello, *Awareness: A de Mello Spirituality Conference in His Own Words*, edited by J. Francis Stroud (New York: Image Books, 1992), p. 144.

6. Vaillant, *Natural History of Alcoholism*, pp. 313–314.

7. *Alcoholics Anonymous*, p. 85.

8. Ibid., p. 84.

9. Shunryu Suzuki, *Zen Mind, Beginner's Mind* (New York: Weatherhill, 1970), p. 32.

10. See the entry under "Temptation" in the editors' Glossary to *The Philokalia*, translated and edited by G. E. H. Palmer, Phillip Sherrard, and Kallistos Ware, vol. I (London: Faber and Faber, 1979), pp. 365–367.

11. Cf. de Mello, *Awareness*, pp. 15–16.

12. Meister Eckhart, "On Detachment," in *Meister Eckhart: The Essential Sermons, Commentaries, Treatises, and Defense*, translated by Edmund Colledge and Bernard McGinn (New York: Paulist Press, 1981).

13. For an excellent discussion of the connection between Eckhart and Heidegger, see John D. Caputo, *The Mystical Element in Heidegger's Thought* (Athens Ohio: Ohio University Press, 1978).

14. Martin Heidegger, "Memorial Address," in *Discourse on Thinking*, translated by John M. Anderson and E. Hans Freund (New York: Harper & Row, 1966).

15. *Alcoholics Anonymous*, p. xiii.

16. In *Addiction and Grace* Gerald May already clearly identified "detachment" as the opposite of addiction.

17. Ibid., p. 164.

18. J. P. de Caussade, *Abandonment to Divine Providence* (Exeter: The Catholic Records Press, 1921).

Chapter 11: Addiction and Responsibility

1. Christopher Lasch, *The True and Only Heaven: Progress and Its Critics* (New York: W. W. Norton, 1991), pp. 518–519.

2. Perrin, *I Am an Adult*, p. 35.

3. That gives the title to one important study of AA: Ernest Kurtz, *Not-God: A History of Alcoholics Anonymous* (Center City, Minn.: Hazelden, 1979).

Index